A Path of Practice

THE BODHI PATH PROGRAM

by Shamar Rinpoche
edited by Tina Draszczyk

Also by Shamar Rinpoche

A Path of Practice

THE BODHI PATH PROGRAM

by Shamar Rinpoche

Edited by Tina Draszczyk

RABSEL
PUBLICATIONS

Photo of Shamar Rinpoche: ©Boris Kaip

RABSEL PUBLICATIONS
16, rue de Babylone
76430 La Remuée, France
www.rabsel.com
contact@rabsel.com

This project was supported by the DRAC and Normandy Region under the FADEL Normandie, France.

© Rabsel Publications, La Remuée, France, 2020
ISBN: 978-2-36017-019-7

Table of Contents

Preface by Jigme Rinpoche

I am very happy that *A Path of Practice: The Bodhi Path Program* has now been made accessible by Tina Draszczyk and Rabsel Éditions.

For more than five decades, the 14th Künzig Shamarpa (1952–2014) took full responsibility as the lineage holder of the Karma Kagyü, or Kamtsang Kagyü, tradition to safeguard its precious and living Dharma methods. Regularly giving detailed Dharma teachings all over the world, organizing and supervising Buddhist monasteries and Dharma centers, offering sutric and tantric Dharma transmissions, he had at heart that the Buddha's methods could be used and applied in our world and in our modern society. In this regard, he organized study programs and supported and instructed meditators both in Asia and the West.

During a one-week course in Germany in 2004, Shamar Rinpoche offered his vision for focused Dharma practice with the power to lead the modern practitioner toward achieving the state of awakening. He called this system the "Bodhi Path," a spiritual path toward bodhi, or awakening. The associated program was offered and organized by Shamar Rinpoche in North America, Asia, and Europe.

For those who wish to seriously walk the path of meditation, Shamar Rinpoche recommends a systematic way of Dharma practice, which he lays out in Part I: "The Bodhi Path Meditation Program." Over the years, Shamar Rinpoche repeatedly stressed that for these meditation practices to be successful, Dharma practitioners require a right view and understanding of the Buddha's teachings. It is in this sense that he also recommends practitioners to delve into the Buddha Dharma by learning the main Buddhist principles in terms of the Buddhist views of reality, ethics, and conduct, the theoretical background of meditation, as well as the precise methods and their application. An overview regarding the entire curriculum, including this study program, is presented in Part II: "The Bodhi Path Curriculum: Studies and Meditation, a Summary."

Shamar Rinpoche's deep and vast knowledge of the Buddha Dharma, his profound realization, and his decades of experience in teaching and guiding people from different walks of life make his recommendations for Dharma practice in today's world a particularly precious source of inspiration. Please feel encouraged to study and apply it to your own Dharma practice. This will bring great benefits to all those who wish to free their mind and progress toward awakening.

Jigme Rinpoche

Landrevie
29 April 2019

Note by the editor

It is a great joy that this book in which Künzig Shamar Rinpoche describes his vision of the Bodhi Path-Program in a clear and well-structured way is now published.

Part I consists of an edited version of teachings that Shamar Rinpoche gave in Remetschwiel, Germany, from 11 to 19 August 2004. Throughout the editing process, I tried to adhere as closely as possible to Rinpoche's lively presentations (he taught in English) while removing some of the repetition. Headings and subheadings were inserted to facilitate the navigation through these teachings. During this week, Shamar Rinpoche answered many questions in relation to the different topics he presented. These questions and answers were repositioned during the editing process so that all questions concerning one topic, for example, the practice of calm abiding (shiné), are now found in one place, i.e., following the detailed instructions on shiné. The sequence of questions and answers therefore does not necessarily follow the original sequence of the course.

Shamar Rinpoche provided additional elucidation and support for the Bodhi Path program in books that he completed subsequent to this seminar in 2004. The reader will find helpful guidance in these books, including *Boundless Awakening, The Path to Awakening,* and *Boundless Wisdom.*

Part II consists of an overview of the entire Bodhi Path curriculum in terms of meditation and studies. This is what you will find on the Bodhi Path websites. In this overview, the meditation practices are divided into (a) core practices, (b) additional practices, and (c) practices to be specially chosen for individuals according to their qualities and aptitudes. In this overview, special emphasis is given to *lojong,* the Mahāyāna practice of mind training. In Part I, you will find the context for this meditation practice as well as for the other practices recommended in a–c.

The endnotes were compiled by myself for those who may not be familiar with the cited names and topics.

As the exact transliteration of the Tibetan is difficult to read by all those who are not familiar with the (Wylie) system, a simple phonetic version of the Tibetan words is used when shown within the main text, while the precise transliteration is offered in the endnotes. Because Sanskrit and Tibetan terms appear frequently throughout this book, they are rendered in italics only on first appearance, and when being emphasized or defined. The term Mahāmudrā is always capitalized.

My thanks go to Isa Duffy for additional English editing as well as to Christoph von Pohl and Jim Baston for their careful proofreading.

Part I

The Bodhi Path Meditation Program

Introduction

BACKGROUND OF THE BODHI PATH MEDITATION PROGRAM

The Kagyü lineage transmits the practice of the so-called Six Yogas of Nāropa,[1] tracing back to Tilopa and passed down through Nāropa, Marpa, Milarepa, and Gampopa,[2] as well as the particular Mahāmudrā lineage transmitted from Saraha through Nāgārjuna, Śavaripa, Maitrīpa,[3] Marpa, Milarepa, and Gampopa. Gampopa taught this latter aspect of Mahāmudrā extensively and combined it with Atiśa's *lojong* practice. This special lineage of Gampopa became known as "the combined lineage of Kadampa and Mahāmudrā".[4] It is one of the main streams of teachings of all Kagyüpas and the particular practice of most lamas who attained enlightenment in the framework of the Kagyü tradition.

Within the Karma Kagyü lineage,[5] this system of Mahāmudrā practice[6] is taught based on various commentaries written by different Karmapas and other Karma

Kagyü masters. It was the 9th Karmapa[7] in particular who composed three treatises on Mahāmudrā: a concise, a medium, and an extensive text. The concise text is called *Mahāmudrā, the Finger Pointing at the Dharmakāya*.[8] The medium text is called *Mahāmudrā, Eliminating the Darkness of Ignorance*.[9] The extensive text is called *Mahāmudrā, the Ocean of Definitive Meaning*.[10]

When engaging in the practice of Mahāmudrā, some practitioners need the support of the above-mentioned Six Yogas of Nāropa, in particular *tummo*[11], to speed up their Mahāmudrā realization. Other practitioners do not; it depends on the individual. Many Kagyü lamas did not require such support and attained their realization simply based on Saraha's Mahāmudrā practice. In its origin, Mahāmudrā is a Sanskrit word in the context of the tantras, and the tantric practice associated with Mahāmudrā in particular is the practice of tummo.

Saraha's Mahāmudrā lineage, also known as the practice of "Pointing Out Mind's Nature", is very profound. This method points precisely to the nature of the mind and leads the practitioner in that training in a very special way. Saraha traveled as a beggar. He gave Mahāmudrā instructions by singing songs and accompanied himself on his string instrument. In his songs, he elucidated the nature of the mind, and many who listened to these songs became enlightened by virtue of Saraha's blessing. They were able to attain the first level of realization on the Mahāmudrā path, which is equivalent to the first *bhūmi*, the first level of a realized bodhisattva. Saraha's teachings came down to us in three *Dohās* (songs) called the *King Dohā*, the *Queen Dohā*, and the *People Dohā*. Saraha's Mahāmudrā teachings are transmitted in two ways: through written instructions, covering only the surface and thus being limited in scope, and through oral key instructions.

To get started, in addition to receiving instructions from a teacher, practitioners may also read books on Mahāmudrā, yet only those who reach a more advanced level in their meditation will receive the so-called oral Mahāmudrā key instructions, which are kept secretly. There is a reason for this. If they were written down and made public, people would naturally be drawn to meditate on what they have read. Their meditation would then be guided by their own imagination and as such could not be accurate. This would also mean that the key points of Mahāmudrā would be distorted or altered, serving no purpose to anyone. In order to avoid this, these oral key instructions have been kept secret. The path of Mahāmudrā thus begins with a student receiving some instructions from a book, from private teachings, or from public seminars. The student should make sure that he or she understands the practice properly. Once one has a good understanding of the path, one should follow it and practice as instructed. According to one's personal progress, the respective teacher will give the more profound instructions when it is deemed appropriate and fitting. Until now, the foundation for these teachings has been very well laid, for example, by the 16th Gyalwa Karmapa, Kalu Rinpoche, and Gendün Rinpoche, who taught on Buddhism in general, on refuge, on bodhicitta and the associated vow, on Mahāyāna lojong, the Six Yogas of Nāropa, and the associated preliminary practices (ngöndro). Yet Saraha's Mahāmudrā teachings have so far not been fully taught in the West.

The tantric aspect of this Mahāmudrā practice is often combined with the Four-Armed Chenrezig (Sanskr.:

Avalokiteśvara), the Two-Armed Chenrezig, or with Chakrasamvara (Tib.: Demchog). With respect to the Four-Armed Chenrezig, i.e., Jinasagara (Tib.: Gyalwa Gyamtso), there are two: white and red. The Mahāmudrā practice associated with the Two-Armed and the Four-Armed white Chenrezig is combined with Mahā Ati (Tib.: Dzog Chen). The Mahāmudrā practice associated with Chakrasamvara and the Red Chenrezig is Mahāmudrā alone, without Mahā Ati. When a disciple arrives at a certain stage, his or her teacher will select a *yidam*[12] for the disciple according to the individual's qualities. The disciple will then engage in the Mahāmudrā practice according to the yidam chosen. When I first organized this Bodhi Path practice, I did a number of predictions to determine which yidam would be suitable for the disciples in general. Every time the result showed me that the White Avalokiteśvara which combines Mahāmudrā and Mahā Ati would be most suitable.

In Tibet there were many transmission lineages for the practice on the White Avalokiteśvara. There is, for example, the lineage of Songtsen Gampo, the so-called Bodhisattva King of Tibet (7th c.). There is another lineage of Guru Padmasambhava,[13] and there are further transmissions from Sakya[14] and Kagyü masters. The 9th Karmapa combined all these lineages into one. The Karma Kagyü's White Avalokiteśvara lineage thus is a combination of virtually all lineages of the White Avalokiteśvara that were transmitted during his time in Tibet. One great bodhisattva of the Karma Kagyü lineage was Karma Chagme.[15] He taught the 9th Karmapa's White Avalokiteśvara combined with Mahāmudrā and Mahā Ati, a practice that became very popular among Kagyü, Nyingma, and also Sakya practitioners. In fact, most of the genuine meditators of the Kagyü and Nyingma schools applied the Mahāmudrā/ Mahā Ati practice associated with the White Chenrezig as their main or heart practice. They still engaged in other meditations, for example, guru yoga on Padmasambhava, Milarepa, or on a Karmapa, and they still continued to receive teachings and initiations on many yidam practices, but ultimately they chose and kept this combination practice of White Avalokiteśvara and Mahāmudrā/Mahā Ati as their core practice.

THE BODHI PATH MEDITATION PROGRAM IN SHORT

My recommendation for the sequence of practices that culminate in Mahāmudrā is:

Common Mahāyāna practices:

o   Refuge and bodhisattva vow.
o   Calm abiding meditation (Tib.: *shiné*, Sanskr.: śamatha) with the support of focusing on the breathing in three levels: (1) counting the breathing cycles, (2) following the breath, and (3) abiding on the breath.
o   Accompanying preliminaries for purifying the mind: prostrations while reciting the *Sūtra of the Thirty-five Buddhas*.[16] During the time period when one practices the prostrations, one also engages in the above-mentioned three levels of shiné practice.
o   Accompanying preliminaries for generating merit: maṇḍala offerings based on the *Sūtra of the Thirty-five Buddhas*. During the time period when one practices the maṇḍala offerings, one also engages in the lojong shiné practice of tonglen meditation, i.e., "giving and taking".

o   Accompanying preliminaries for receiving blessing: guru yoga with Chenrezig, a practice in the tradition of Tangtong Gyalpo.[17]

Mahāmudrā practice in the context of the common Mahāyāna path:

o   Combined with calm abiding, one focuses on the practice of deep insight (Tib.: *lhagthong*, Sanskr.: *vipaśyanā*), first based on exploring mind's true nature, then by directly abiding in it. These two aspects of deep insight meditation are mutually supportive.

o   In addition, one focuses on the Chenrezig guru yoga practice. This will lead to the full awakening of buddhahood.

Mahāmudrā practice in the context of the uncommon Mahāyāna path:

o   If you wish to practice the Vajrayāna, the Dorje Sempa recitation (Vajrasattva) is applied as an additional preliminary practice after having received the empowerment.

o   During the time period when one practices the Dorje Sempa recitation, one can also engage in the lojong shiné practice of tonglen meditation and the analytical type of lhagthong practice.

o   Finally, you start with the elaborated type of the Chenrezig yidam practice. Having received the empowerment, one first focuses on the generation process. This is followed by the practice of the perfection process,[18] which combines Mahāmudrā and Mahā Ati, a practice culminating in the full awakening of buddhahood.

(Note by the editor: Shamar Rinpoche provided additional elucidation and support for the Bodhi Path program in books that he
completed subsequent to this seminar in 2004. The reader will
also find helpful guidance in these books, including *Boundless
Awakening, The Path to Awakening,* and *Boundless Wisdom.*)

A Systematic Approach for Successful Dharma Practice

AN OVERVIEW: THE PRACTICE OF THE MAHĀYĀNA PATH

To be successful in the Dharma practice of Mahāyāna Buddhism aimed at attaining the state of complete and perfect awakening, you need to walk the path of Dharma. This path consists of two levels: the common path and the uncommon path. Without the support of the common path, you can never reach the uncommon path. Thus, if you wish to practice the uncommon path, you have to rely on the common path first. This means that you have to practice both.

Whether or not someone will encounter the uncommon path depends on the individual practitioner's karma. If your karma is very conducive for the path to full awakening, you will walk the uncommon path. If your karma is generally positive and if, in this sense, you have a good foundation, you will be able to connect with the common path. On this basis, you will eventually also encounter the uncommon path.

The Common Mahāyāna Path

Refuge and bodhicitta

With respect to the common path, you need the refuge and bodhisattva vows.

Refuge can be compared to a solid foundation. To take refuge means to take refuge in the Buddha, the Dharma, and the Sangha, which is the first and fundamental level of Dharma practice. It acts like a fertile ground. When you want something to grow, you first need to clear the soil and fertilize it. Likewise, with respect to the attaining of enlightenment, you first have to purify your mind of its ignorance and to develop the path of Dharma from within yourself. Taking refuge affords you a very important foundation for this process.

The bodhisattva vow is like a staircase. In a many-storied house, you cannot reach any of the higher levels without a staircase, which makes this a perfect metaphor for the bodhisattva vow with its two aspects: relative bodhicitta and absolute bodhicitta. Relative bodhicitta is like the foundation for the staircase, and absolute bodhicitta is like its steps. Relative bodhicitta comprises the attitude of loving kindness and compassion toward all sentient beings. As long as this attitude is dualistic in nature, it is relative bodhicitta. Absolute bodhicitta is the non-dual wisdom of the bodhicitta mind, while relative bodhicitta is connected to emotional states of mind and therefore quite limited in scope. As long as the compassion and loving kindness of relative bodhicitta are lacking the wisdom of absolute bodhicitta, you will naturally be attached, and you will grasp. The effect is that many emotions will be stirred up, which in itself shows that this level of bodhicitta is not yet pure. Nevertheless, relative bodhicitta is the indispensable basis for absolute bodhicitta or wisdom. In other words, you have to develop the absolute bodhicitta mind from the ground of relative bodhicitta. *Bodhi* means "awakening"; *bodhicitta* means "the heart of awakening". *Bodhi Path* means "the path to awakening", and on the path of bodhi, one's heart should eventually be detached from any dualistic emotions. This is why the view of absolute bodhicitta is required on the Bodhi Path.

As for developing absolute bodhicitta, there are a few steps to go through. The first step is to listen to the precise instructions about the nature of phenomena. The teachings of the Buddha explain precisely how phenomena are just illusions of your mind. On a relative level, everything is there as you see it. However, the absolute or ultimate nature of any outer and inner phenomenon is that they do not *truly* exist. Take the beams of a house, for example. They are supported by the pillars, and the pillars in turn stand on the ground. We can say that the beams depend on the pillars, which in turn depend on the ground. And the roof of the house depends on the beams. Put all these interdependent parts together, and you have a house. This is the relative truth of the house, a collection of many interdependent parts. If you were to look for the absolute truth of the house itself, you do not find it in any of its parts, because the foundation is not the house, the walls are not the house, the pillars are not the house, and the roof and the beams are not the house. Thus, in absolute or ultimate truth, the house does not truly exist, while, relatively, everything exists in an interdependent way. In this sense, right now you are in the relative existence of saṃsāra. If you wish to liberate yourself from saṃsāra, you will have to depend on the Dharma comprising both relative and absolute bodhicitta. These are all the "parts" that you need in order to build your "house of awakening".

Thus, by relying on the path of Dharma, which is the relative truth, you will reach the ultimate truth of awakening, which is the state of mind when all ignorance of your mind has dissipated. This is the final, ultimate truth. Yet, conventionally, you need a path to get there; you need a path that can clear away ignorance. The path is relative. It is required so long as you are travelling to your destination, just like you need all the parts to build a house. As long as delusion persists, you need the remedies to counteract them until you fully recover from your delusion. On this path, you come to understand the problems of the mind, and you also come to know which remedies to apply in order to solve these problems. Thus, solving the problems depends on applying the relevant remedy. Therefore, as long as you know the problem, you also know the remedy. This is the relative path for ultimate awakening.

Sentient beings are totally fettered by the problems that continue in relative reality; it is delusion, which makes for the relatively existing saṃsāra, the realms of living beings. There is no ultimately existing saṃsāra. *Ultimate* implies something unchanging. This does not hold true for saṃsāra, which is just relative and like a dream and thus can be eliminated. If saṃsāra existed in an ultimate sense, it could never be removed. If a dream truly existed, it would not disappear even when you wake up. Because a dream itself has no real existence, it disappears naturally upon waking. The dream has not gone off somewhere, and you do not put it away in some corner and walk away. The dream itself does not exist and therefore vanishes when you wake up. The processes of saṃsāra consists of all the negative emotions and karma. It is based on ignorance, which gives rise to negative emotions. The thereby accrued karma uninterruptedly displays the illusions of saṃsāra, and all these conditions depend on and feed on each other. Together, they are experienced as saṃsāra. Yet nothing truly exists. Ultimate awakening is ultimate truth. All samsaric problems can be solved because they are illusory and not the ultimate truth. When ultimate enlightenment is attained, saṃsāra comes to an end!

Within the various types of samsaric existence, this human life is considered as extremely precious, and Buddhist teachings introduce you to the understanding of how precious your life is. A human life has the full potential and capacity to turn toward awakening, to know all the paths leading to it, and to be able to walk on these paths to get there. A human life has wisdom; it has potential, opportunity. The human mind is rich enough to understand the path to awakening, to understand the meaning of ultimate bodhicitta, i.e., that, and how, all phenomena do not *truly* exist. For that, however, you first have to listen to the teachings of the Buddha and how he explained the ultimate nature of phenomena. The second step is that you have to think about it over and over again to understand the actual meaning. Then the third step, the path of meditation, will become clear to you. So listen to the teachings, reflect on them, and then meditate. These are the steps of the path of Dharma. Your capacity to absorb the most profound meaning of the Dharma depends on your reflecting on the teachings.

All living beings are caught in the trap of clinging. Based on the clinging to a self, one also clings to other things in many ways, wanting this and that. Meditation has been designed so that you can naturally dissolve this chain of clinging, which is nothing but a distortion created by your samsaric mind; it is not how the mind as such actually is. The process of meditation is therefore a way to clear up these chains of clinging.

There are two types of clinging: the clinging to samsaric phenomena and, on a more advanced level, the clinging to the path of Dharma. The latter is also a problem. Your precise understanding and view of absolute bodhicitta, emptiness, Madhyamaka, i.e., being free from the four extremes and the eight elaborations,[19] can remove both types of clinging.

In any case, first comes the refuge vow. On its basis, the bodhisattva vow, with its relative and ultimate perspectives, may be taken. The relative bodhisattva vow is taken as a commitment, in that you commit yourself to uphold the relative bodhicitta mind of loving kindness and compassion. The ultimate aspect of the bodhisattva vow is more than a vow; it means to actually develop the wisdom of bodhicitta mind.

Shiné/śamatha: the practice of calm abiding, first steps

On the basis of taking refuge and the bodhisattva vow, you first engage in the practice of calm abiding. In general, there are six levels of the so-called common shiné practice based on the support of the breath; they range from coarse to subtle. In the Bodhi Path meditation system, the

24

recommendation is to go through the first three of these six levels, that is, focusing the mind by: (1) counting the breathing cycles, (2) following the breath, and (3) abiding on the breath. The subtler levels (4–6) are not necessarily required, because in the Bodhi Path meditation program I recommend continuing on this basis with the Mahāmudrā type of lhagthong/vipaśyanā meditation.[20]

The practice of calm abiding aims at training the mind to become free from the bad habit of constant, busy thinking and the confusion that goes along with it. It is similar to taming a wild horse. With this training, your mind will become free from its preoccupations. The common shiné practice thus trains your mind to become stable. The stability of your shiné will depend on your own diligence. If you maintain your shiné practice consistently, the state of calm abiding will become your nature; it is not something that you bring into your mind newly. By virtue of the advanced type of shiné practice, you will develop an unobstructed peace of mind, an open mind serving as the ground to develop the realization of emptiness. This realization, which comprises both the essencelessness of a self-identity and the essencelessness of phenomena in general, is like the eyes of meditation on the path to awakening. To develop these two eyes, that is, realizing the two aspects of essencelessness, one needs a stable mind. It is through the practice of shiné that one develops this stability.

Someone who has achieved a very strong basis in shiné has the necessary foundation to develop the realization of the emptiness of phenomena and of mind. These two eyes are what is called the view. It is not a view that you can learn from books but rather one that you have to experience. With these two eyes in your experience, you will be able to look at your mind, examine each of your negative emotions, and thereby clear up all the ignorance of your mind. As Śāntideva says in his *Bodhicaryāvatāra*[21] (VIII.4):

> Understanding that deep insight that is
> fully supported by calm abiding
> will fully vanquish all the defilements,
> you should first seek calm abiding, which
> in turn is accomplished by delighting in
> the freedom from worldly attachments.

You will develop this level of shiné successfully if you are not terribly attached to things. It does not mean that you should not own a car. It does not mean not to enjoy your breakfast. It simply means not to emotionally grasp for it. Tilopa taught Nāropa, "My son, it is not the things that fetter you, but your attachment to them." The chain is not what you see, but your grasping at it. This is why reducing emotional grasping is a good condition to develop shiné and thus the foundation to develop the precise view of lhagthong, or deep insight.

Accompanying preliminaries for purifying the mind: *The Practice of the Sūtra of the Thirty-five Buddhas and prostrations*

The practice of shiné, which subdues the mind's confusion and its restlessness, is taught first so that wisdom can eventually develop. Yet there is another problem in your mind, another obscuration that needs to be addressed. It is the problem of negative karma. Therefore, when you engage in shiné practice, I recommend that you also practice the preliminaries[22] based on the *Sūtra of the Thirty-five*

Buddhas. Prostrations are practiced in order to purify one-self of negative karma. All four schools of Tibetan Buddhism embrace the lineage of this practice. In the Kagyü tradition, Marpa, the Great Translator, applied the Preliminaries based on this practice of the *Sūtra of the Thirty-five Buddhas.*[23] It would be best to practice sequentially the three levels of common shiné, that is, focusing the mind with the support of the breath by: (1) counting the breathing cycles, (2) following the breath, and (3) abiding on the breath, and to accomplish a calm state of mind during the time period while you are practicing one hundred thousand prostrations. Then you start with the next step of the preliminary practices, i.e., the maṇḍala offerings. While this would be the best way to go about the practice, it is not necessarily fixed. Whether shiné, i.e., a calm mind, is accomplished or not, is evident from your state of mind. If your mind is still busy, you have to continue with the three basic levels of shiné mentioned above. Your own experience will tell you when your mind has achieved the effect of shiné meditation. There is no need to obtain confirmation from somebody else. When you attain the result of shiné, it is recommended that you shift your further shiné practice to the lojong shiné practice of tonglen meditation, i.e., "giving and taking".

Accompanying preliminaries for generating merit: *The Practice of the Sūtra of the Thirty-five Buddhas and maṇḍala offerings*

The preliminary practices continue with the maṇḍala practice in the visualized presence of these Thirty-five Buddhas in order to accumulate the power of merit, which is required for successfully engaging in the Mahāyāna path of Dharma. Thus, with prostrations you purified yourself of karma, and now, with the maṇḍala offerings, you are gathering the support of merit. Bodhisattvas who wish to be of benefit to sentient beings depend on this accumulation of merit. Merit in turn depends on giving. The practice of the maṇḍala offerings allows you to mentally practice generosity. It is a kind of mental therapy. You visualize, or think of, all the things that you are attached to. Then you release your clinging by offering them. You mentally give away all these things. This way you are developing the attitude of giving everything away, which is a very meritorious practice. At present, you don't have so many things to give to sentient beings. Your capacity to give to others depends on your karma. Here, the first step is to mentally give away everything, which means you will accumulate the merit of generosity in your mind. By practicing generosity, you might become a very wealthy bodhisattva, able to give an abundance of things to sentient beings in order to benefit them. Alongside the maṇḍala offerings, it would be best to also start with the practice of lojong shiné practice (tonglen meditation), i.e., "giving and taking". This is a type of shiné practice that also incorporates the perspective of lhagthong, or deep insight.

Shiné of "giving and taking": lojong, the practice of Mahāyāna mind training

Once your mind has gained stability based on the common shiné practice, you will proceed with the lojong practice of giving and taking, or tonglen, which is a more advanced type of shiné practice and actually comprises both shiné and lhagthong. With the maṇḍala offering, you generate a lot of merit. Engaging in the lojong practice of "giving and taking" during this time means that you really have something to send to sentient beings. Lojong is a bodhisattva practice where you give your happiness to sentient beings and take on their suffering. It is effective in accumulating very powerful merit and will thereby greatly enhance your practice of calm abiding. In this way, you will definitely be able to achieve very good experiences of shiné. This result will happen naturally because the greater the purification of negative karma, the more luminous and clearer your mind. Thus, your shiné will develop more and more, and you will become very familiar with a calm state of mind. Eventually, your stability of mind will become very mature.[24]

Accompanying preliminaries for receiving blessing: *Guru yoga with Chenrezig*

After the maṇḍala offerings and along with the lojong shiné practice of "giving and taking", in order to receive blessing, you can also practice the guru yoga type of Chenrezig practice according to the lineage of Tangtong Gyalpo.

Lhagthong/vipaśyanā: the practice of deep insight, culminating in Mahāmudrā

On this basis, your shiné will be excellent, which means that you will be ready to receive and properly apply the lhagthong teachings to explore mind's true nature. This lhagthong practice comprises two levels: the analytical level, where you examine the mind, and the level of directly abiding in mind's true nature. If you have attained good shiné, you will be able to practice this very successfully.

The first step, i.e., analytical lhagthong, is a preliminary level on the path of Mahāmudrā. In this practice, mind's true nature is explored, for example, by dividing the mind into three aspects: the past mind, the present mind, and the future mind. This is one way to explore the mind as such. If you have a good level of shiné, you can do this practice very comfortably, and it is very effective. On this basis, you will proceed with the Mahāmudrā type of lhagthong, directly abiding in mind's nature. Based on the stability of mind resulting from shiné, you will be successful in these different steps of lhagthong, culminating in the uncommon Mahāmudrā type of lhagthong.[25]

The Uncommon Mahāyāna Path

Additional preliminaries

The Dorje Sempa (Vajrasattva) practice

If you wish to practice the Vajrayāna you will, then, while you engage in lojong shiné and the preliminary analytical lhagthong practice, also be given the empowerment for Dorje Sempa (Sanskr.: Vajrasattva) and engage in the associated practice for a certain period of time. During the time you are engaging in the Dorje Sempa practice, you may not need to practice the Chenrezig Sādhanā of Tangtong Gyalpo, because then you have Dorje Sempa to relate to.

The generation and perfection processes of Chenrezig (Avalokiteśvara)

On this basis, you can engage in the Chenrezig practice on the level of the Highest Yogatantra (Sanskr.: Yoganiruttaratantra), which is a powerful practice. Beforehand, however, you have to receive the elaborate empowerment for the yidam practice of Chenrezig. This kind of Vajrayāna practice generally comprises two phases, the so-called generation and perfection processes. The perfection process consists of Mahāmudrā meditation as such. To begin with, however, you focus on the generation process for which you will be given the related instructions. They concern, firstly, the empowerment and how to receive it; secondly, the *samayas*, or precepts, that protect the Vajrayāna practice; and thirdly, the purpose of the generation process.

Generally speaking, the generation process, that is, the visualization of the yidam and so on, is the so-called uncommon type of shiné practice. In the Vajrayāna, shiné practice is incorporated by way of focusing the mind on certain visualizations, which will enhance the quality of your stability in shiné. Yet without having first been trained in the ordinary way of common shiné as pointed out above, you will not be able to properly engage in the generation process.

The perfection process of this Chenrezig practice comprise a combination of Mahāmudrā and Mahā Ati.[26] This combination of Chenrezig practice with Mahāmudrā and Mahā Ati culminates in the full awakening of buddhahood.

With this I have given you a general overview of the direction of the meditation teachings offered in the Bodhi Path Buddhist Centers. Now the way is laid out for you so

that you can tap into your potential to achieve enlightenment within one lifetime. The systematic programs available to you at the Bodhi Path centers will provide you with
the necessary teachings and guidance.

DETAILED INSTRUCTIONS: THE PRACTICE OF THE COMMON MAHĀYĀNA PATH, FIRST STEPS

Some General Advice Regarding Listening to Dharma Teachings

First of all, when you listen to dharma teachings, you have
to know that you are listening to a subject that has an
entirely different cultural background than the one you
are familiar with in Western culture. Secondly, when you
listen to dharma teachings, apply your common sense and
logic in order to assess, investigate, and truly understand
the teachings. The Buddha Dharma will also teach you certain ways of logical reasoning. Learning these will improve
your capacity to understand the subject. All this will help
you to understand. It will help you to not relate to these
teachings only from an already established Western point
of view. It might also help you to be less irritated by unfa-
miliar concepts or not to feel disappointed when you notice that certain Buddhist views do not go along the lines
of Western thinking.

As you listen to these Buddhist teachings, you may become excited and think, "Oh, this is what I always thought."
You might be a person who is very critical of Western
concepts and the Western way of life, and you may even
degrade Western culture. Coming in contact with, for ex-

ample, certain Hindu or Buddhist views might feel like a confirmation of your own views. You then continue to use these new concepts to further degrade the Western concepts, which could lead to a lot of confusion. Let's take an admittedly extreme example: you meet a Hindu sadhu who goes naked and you hear that Milarepa was also naked. If you think that in the West nakedness is dealt with in a too prudish way, you might now feel confirmed and think, "I always knew it was right to walk around naked." Thus, you would just use certain aspects, which also have to be seen in their cultural perspective, to support your deluded concepts.

Another example: the medieval church often made people feel guilty and pressured them to confess their sins. As you hear about karma and the associated purification practices, some of you might reject this teaching because it reminds you of that, overlooking the point that the Buddhist concept in this regard is quite different from the Christian one. Rejecting this aspect of Buddhism on the spot might also indicate that you don't have the flexibility to learn and that you are simply stuck in your own view. All this might lead to serious misunderstandings. Some of you might also be comforted by the impression that the Christian emphasis on sin, guilt, and associated punishment is confirmed by Buddhist views. This will then encourage you to identify with your feelings of guilt. Others might think that these Buddhist teachings are of no value as they are just the same as the Christian views about guilt, and so on. In terms of the Buddhist view, both versions are serious misunderstandings.

Therefore, be aware that you are learning a new subject. There is some similarity to concepts the Western world is familiar with, yet many views are different. Think about what you hear and reflect on it in order to get a more accurate understanding. Also, be careful in the way you assess the wording. For example, the Buddha taught a sūtra to a female disciple who apparently was a very beautiful woman. She asked a number of questions, and the Buddha answered each by saying, "Beautiful woman, beautiful woman, it is like that . . . , it is like that . . ." He always addressed her as "beautiful woman". Suppose the translator of this sūtra was, for example, an American. He or she might right away conclude that the Buddha was a very sexist person and disapprove of him. This extreme type of sensitivity can create a lot of unnecessary problems in one's mind. Be careful in this regard, and more open.

Refuge in Buddha, Dharma, and Sangha

Buddha

"Buddha" means to be free from all veils that have obscured the mind and to have developed all qualities inherent to the mind. This is the state of being fully and perfectly awakened; it is the dharmakāya, also referred to as the perfected benefit of oneself.

Generally speaking, obscurations are distinguished into three types: (1) afflicting obscurations, (2) cognitive obscurations, and (3) the subtle obscurations of habitual patterns. Having overcome the first type of obscuration means that one has achieved liberation from saṃsāra, the ongoing cycle of existence. Having overcome the second type of obscuration means that, as a bodhisattva, one has transcended this kind of self-liberation as well. Having overcome the third type of obscuration means one has accomplished the state of being fully and perfectly awakened.

Look at Buddha Śākyamuni, who had been practicing as a bodhisattva for a very long time. In peoples' perceptions, he did not appear as an enlightened being from the very beginning. He was a prince and enjoyed his life. Then, at a certain point, he realized that there was no true meaning in the life of a king, no actual satisfaction. Consequently, he searched for the cause of true happiness and understood that it consists in freeing the mind from its ignorance. With this aim, he renounced everything, went to the forest, and meditated. With meditation, he became able to overcome all of these three types of obscuration and attained the state of being fully awakened; this is the *dharmakāya*. Yet this did not mean that he simply disappeared. Buddha, the state of being awakened, naturally manifests continuously for the benefit of sentient beings.

During his lifetime as Buddha Śākyamuni, he taught sentient beings the path toward awakening. Thousands and thousands of disciples traversed this path. Yet such activity is not limited to just one lifetime. In fact, a buddha's activity manifests constantly and spontaneously. For ex-ample, when the sun rises, the sunlight appears in every spot of water—likewise, the spontaneous manifestation of buddhahood appear everywhere, in every realm, for the benefit of sentient beings. *Buddha* means "awakened", completely. A buddha has attained this state based on the bodhisattva practice. A bodhisattva has generated compassion for sentient beings and has engaged in wishes to support sentient beings. With the attainment of buddhahood, all these wishes naturally fulfill themselves through all kinds of manifestations that are perceptible to sentient beings, the so-called *nirmāṇakāyas*. A buddha's emanations can even manifest in the form of insects, helping these tiny sentient beings. To be sure, the real cause of liberation from saṃsāra is your own mind. It is your own mind that has to change from an ignorant mode to a state free from all delusion. Yet, you can receive help from the nirmāṇakāyas that encourage sentient beings to transform their state of mind. In the case of insects, this encouragement has to come from an insect; humans cannot encourage insects to change their state of mind. Thus, nirmāṇakāya is the word used to label the buddhas' various beneficial manifestations attuned to different samsaric sentient beings. The nirmāṇakāyas are what sentient beings can perceive in their impure worlds, with their impure minds.

There are also beings who are already highly developed: realized bodhisattvas who have attained the bodhisattva levels, or bhūmis. Yet they still need support to cross all the bhūmis in order to reach full enlightenment. As their mind is very pure, they can perceive buddha manifestations on a very pure level, in extremely beautiful forms, such as Vajradhara. These are called *sambhogakāya*, and they also manifest due to the buddhas' wishes. The bodhisattvas' pure and clear minds are like a mirror in which the pure and clear reflections of the sambhogakāyas appear.

In this way, nirmāṇakāyas and sambhogakāyas appear according to the states of mind of sentient beings and bodhisattvas. All these manifestations, whether they are nirmāṇakāya or sambhogakāya, are inseparable from the dharmakāya, the state of being fully awakened.

If you describe these three kāyas in another way, you can describe them in terms of wisdom, which is vast and profound. *Dharmakāya* is the word used to denominate *profound* wisdom, because it is one's own deep realization, which cannot be assessed by anyone. *Nirmāṇakāya* and *sambhogakāya* refer to *vast* wisdom, meaning the abundance of supportive manifestations. In fact, vast wisdom is just one aspect of profound wisdom. By virtue of profound wisdom, vast wisdom naturally manifests. Profound wisdom means that the mind is totally free from all three levels of obscuration: coarse, medium, and subtle. Free from all obscurations, the mind has transformed into non-dual, profound wisdom from which vast wisdom manifests. A non-dual mind understands everything—that is, all delusions of sentient beings—as their dreams or states of ignorance. This profound wisdom naturally manifests, according to the respective dreams of sentient beings, as the vast wisdom of the nirmāṇakāyas and sambhogakāyas. This is the meaning of *buddha* and the associated qualities.

Taking refuge in Buddha means to understand and fully appreciate these qualities in order to attain complete and perfect awakening for the benefit of all sentient beings. Thus, Buddha is the ultimate refuge.

Dharma

Dharma comprises two aspects. First, it is the path toward enlightenment, which is also called the "truth of the path". It comprises the entire range of remedies that can eliminate all obscurations. In our world, the Dharma was taught by Buddha Śākyamuni to his disciples. The lineage is unbroken; these teachings still exist in our world. Dharma, which shows the path, may also appear in gestures or as some kinds of examples. The second aspect pertains to the results of having implemented the Dharma methods. This is called the "truth of cessation of suffering". The truth of cessation does not consist of words but is a mental experience that will develop by practicing the Dharma of teachings or the truth of the path. The final truth of cessation is buddha, the state of perfect awakening, and all progressive results accomplished until this ultimate truth of cessation is reached are included in the Dharma of the path.

Taking refuge in the Dharma means that until you are fully enlightened you rely on the path of Dharma. In this sense, taking refuge in the Dharma is temporary.

Sangha

The Sangha has two aspects. The first is the "genuine Sangha", the community of those who are already on advanced levels of the Dharma path, that is, realized beings, be it realized bodhisattvas or realized śrāvakas.[27] In the Theravāda context, the "genuine Sangha" consists of those who are on the path of application and on the path of seeing.[28] They can therefore be on different levels of spiritual development, which one can relate to as small, medium, advanced, and accomplished; they are always either humans or celestial beings.[29] In the Mahāyāna context, the "genuine Sangha" consists of all realized bodhisattvas, all those on the bhūmis; they can appear in any form, even as small ants or butterflies. The second aspect of Sangha consists of what may be called a "semi-sangha". These are practitioners who have renounced worldly life and strive for liberation by listening, reflecting, and meditating. If four members of this semi-sangha come together, they are said to carry a blessing equivalent to that of one member of the genuine Sangha.

Taking refuge in the Sangha means to temporarily take refuge in them as qualified guides on the path of Dharma. When you take refuge in the Sangha of bodhisattvas, in terms of your liberation you take refuge in bodhisattvas who are in human form, because you can communicate with them. For accumulating merit, you can also supplicate to those bodhisattvas who appear in other forms, such as dolphins, for example.

First, you take refuge in the presence of a qualified teacher who represents the Buddha in that he or she introduces you to the Buddha Dharma. As pointed out above, Buddha is the ultimate refuge, while Dharma and Sangha are temporary aspects of refuge. You imagine all buddhas and bodhisattvas in front of you, and prostrate three times, which is a way to show respect to the Buddha, the Dharma, and the Sangha with your body, your speech, and your mind. It also purifies obstacles with respect to your body, speech, and mind. The refuge vow is then taken with genuine devotion to Buddha, Dharma, and Sangha, knowing their qualities. The recitation is repeated three times. During this recitation you say and commit yourself in the following way: "I will now take refuge in Buddha, Dharma, and Sangha until I attain full enlightenment." The teacher then snaps their fingers, at which point you actually receive the refuge vows in a transmission lineage that remained unbroken from the Buddha and which is transmitted from teacher to student. Afterward, some hair is cut to symbolize one's renunciation from saṃsāra. You can learn more detailed instructions on Buddha, Dharma, Sangha, and the precepts that go along with the refuge vow in the Bodhi Path centers.

Becoming a Bodhisattva

Understanding suffering and genuine compassion

The root of enlightenment lies in the development of bodhicitta for sentient beings. In the beginning, you will have a rather emotional type of compassion toward sentient beings by becoming more and more aware of their suffering. Then, as you start to understand the broader picture and the cause of suffering, your compassion will change into wisdom-compassion, which means into non-emotional compassion. The cause of suffering is the ignorance of beings; this ignorance creates suffering, which does not truly exist. It is just an illusion. Ignorance itself is not truly existent either. So, as one comes to know the reality of ignorance, which is that it does not truly exist, ignorance vanishes just like darkness vanishes when the sun rises. The darkness itself doesn't exist; therefore, it can disappear. It is not something that you push away. The sunrise is the development of wisdom within your mind, within the minds of sentient beings, by virtue of which ignorance naturally dissipates.

Suffering is an illusion, and this is precisely the reason why sentimental compassion is not adequate. Suffering is removable; it doesn't really exist. This holds true for any suffering, your own and that of others. In terms of emotions—they do not truly exist either. Moreover, you never experience the emotions of others, but only your own emotions. In fact, it is easy to introduce you to your own emotions—simply because it is your own experience. Thoroughly research your emotions. First try to bring up a particular emotion in your mind, and then examine how it exists. You can examine it thoroughly because it is right there, within you, and you experience it. Explore whether it is in your skin or in your bones or in your blood—in which part of your body is it located? If you search, you will not find any abode, and as you are searching for it, the emotion has disappeared. Where did it go to? Is it hiding somewhere, in a corner of your body? When you examine your negative or positive emotions, you will not find any real existence. Analyze: When somebody causes you to be angry, is your emotion within that person or within yourself? Did he or she throw it on you? Check it! Maybe your anger was switched on by someone else? But then—from where, how exactly, and by whom? Analyze every part of your mind in search of the emotion that you gave rise to, and then examine the emotion itself precisely.

In this way, any emotion can become an object of inquiry. You will discover that none of your emotions truly exist. Rather, you will discover them to be empty, lacking a concrete self-nature. The actual nature of emotions is their emptiness. In this way, by exploring your emotions, you can develop wisdom within yourself. An emotional mind is easy to examine. You can also explore non-emotional thoughts, that is, concepts, and you will discover that the same holds true for them—none of these thoughts truly exist. Thoughts and emotions do not truly exist even though, superficially, they appear clearly, like a mirage or an optical illusion. Thus, when you look at your emotions, like sadness, anxiety, or happiness, you will come to understand that they are just like waves in the mind: when these waves surface, you feel them; when they do not surface in your mind, you do not experience them. You should therefore examine them when you experience them. At this point, when by way of your inquiry you do not find anything, don't become tense, don't push for anything. Just keep the awareness of that. Then, when yet another movement in your mind occurs, examine it again within yourself. It does not make any difference if it is something positive or negative, if it makes you happy or unhappy. Whatever occurs, if you are sad or if you have to cry, just examine what is going on within you. It could happen that you get frightened because there is nothing you can find. In this case, take that fear as an object of your inquiry. This is how by exploring you develop an accurate view of your mind. Through this, you will have a direct experience of the real nature, of the pure aspect, of your mind. And what is more—doing so will enable you to understand that the mind of others works in the same way.

Therefore, all suffering of sentient beings is similar to waves surfacing in their perceptions without any true existence. Everything is just like a mirage or a dream. Everything is similar to reflections that are reflected in mirrors set up in a triangular constellation—multiple reflections. Everything is just a collection of many factors without any solid existence to it.

The meaning of *bodhisattva*

Bodhi translates to the "awakened state"; *sattva* pertains to a "courageous mind directed toward awakening". In this regard, there are slightly different motivations. One of them is the shepherd-like motivation: these bodhisattvas first take care of all sentient beings, just like a shepherd takes care of their sheep, and only after that do they take care of themselves. First, I try to liberate all sentient beings, and then I go for enlightenment for myself. Another kind of bodhisattva is like a king, having the intention to first become a king oneself and to then protect the people. Yet another is like a ferryman, crossing the river together with all the other people on board. These differences happen when the bodhisattva is on the higher path of accumulation and on the path of application[30].

The shepherd-like bodhisattva

When bodhisattvas attain the final level of meditative absorption, or shiné, their mind is very flexible and powerful, very clear and stable. With the support of this stability, they develop *prajñā*, or insight. In this case, prajñā means lhagthong, the meditative absorption in the perfection of wisdom. Even though a bodhisattva at this stage has not yet attained a bodhisattva bhūmi, he or she has already developed a mind of prajñā, which is similar to bright light dispelling the darkness of ignorance. With this prajñā, bodhisattvas are able to eventually overcome the different obscurations. Their prajñā "hits the target". Bodhisattvas thus implement insight with regard to the many different *kleśas*, the emotional afflictions, similar to setting up a spotlight on each of these defilements. Thereby, bodhisattvas know and illuminate each of the defilements by knowing their essence. In this sense, prajñā is like light. Yet bodhisattvas deliberately do not apply this light with regard to a minor level of attachment to the body because bodhisattvas intentionally maintain and use their body and future rebirths. This minor level of attachment to the body is a bit like sexual desire. Generally speaking, according to Buddhism, sexual desire is the cause of rebirth and whether this rebirth will be good or bad depends on karma. In the case of such bodhisattvas, however, this type of attachment has nothing to do with actual sexual desire. They simply and deliberately keep a certain minor level of desire and make wishes to be reborn in saṃsāra in order to benefit sentient beings. To be a bit more precise: the shepherd-like bodhisattva's sexual attachment through which he or she continues to accumulate karma is what propels him or her to rebirths in saṃsāra, and the bodhisattva's wishing prayers are what perfects the rebirth in that they pave the way for the type of body the bodhisattva will have and the environment in which he or she will be reborn. In this way, the bodhisattva is able to take rebirth in saṃsāra again and again. The shepherd-like bodhisattvas want to be in the realms of sentient beings for a long time in order to fulfill their commitment to benefit sentient beings. As far as the above-mentioned minor level of sexual desire is concerned, it doesn't mean they enact this kind of attachment. It rather means that they purposely do not eliminate these tendencies in their minds and instead use it in order to take rebirth. This is very different from the arhats' approach in that the śrāvaka practitioners eliminate everything that causes further rebirths in saṃsāra. Therefore, they completely break through and reach the level of no-more-return to saṃsāra. As these practitioners cut off the cause for rebirth, and therefore do not involve themselves with sentient beings, they also do not accumulate merit because merit depends on how much you help sentient beings. As pointed out before, the shepherd-like bodhisattvas want to be in the realms of sentient beings in order to be very helpful to them. How much they can be of help depends on specific causes. The main causes for becoming truly helpful for sentient beings are one's dedication to a bodhisattva's commitment, one's wish to be helpful, and to involve oneself in helpful actions, ranging from giving food to animals to the practice of unlimited generosity. An important factor bodhisattvas develop in order to become helpful to sentient beings are the bodhisattvas' wishes: "I want to be like this and this in order to be helpful to sentient beings." In his *Bodhicaryāvatāra*, Śāntideva dedicates an entire chapter to the way bodhisattvas make such wishes. Thus, bodhisattvas join the main causes for helping others, that is, dedication and wishes, with the minor level of attachment described above, and are therefore able to spontaneously take rebirth in different realms and be helpful. This is, in fact, very difficult because in the realms of saṃsāra the bodhisattvas will face all kinds of hardship. Helping sentient beings is difficult, right? To be sure, the more skillful you are in meeting these challenges, the more merit you will accumulate. Later, when you attain the bhūmis, your capacity will be more powerful, and with the accomplishment of buddhahood, your capacity to help sentient beings will be unlimited.

The ferryman-like bodhisattva

This type of bodhisattva will not "postpone" achieving the bhūmis. Rather, while they strive to attain realization, they also engage in helping sentient beings. While this type of bodhisattva does not hesitate to face the hardship of helping sentient beings, they will not try to remain in the realm of sentient beings for longer. Helping others and achieving their own development and benefit go together.

The king-like bodhisattva

This type of bodhisattva thinks that he or she cannot be involved in the realms of sentient beings for many millions of eons. Therefore, they apply their prajñā to eliminate all causes for saṃsāra and try to attain the first bhūmi—all the while maintaining the motivation to benefit sentient beings. Thus, having accomplished this realization, they will have the spontaneous power to help sentient beings. They therefore try to reach the first bhūmi more quickly in order to help sentient beings from this powerful position.

The Five Paths: the spiritual development of a bodhisattva

Grounded in bodhicitta, all bodhisattvas proceed on their path toward awakening through the so-called five paths of: (1) accumulation, (2) application, (3) seeing, (4) cultivation, and (5) no-more-learning. The shepherd-like bodhisattvas and the ferryman-like bodhisattvas remain longer on the first two paths. The king-like bodhisattvas try to attain the path of seeing quickly by traversing through the paths of accumulation and application more speedily. The path of seeing is equivalent to the first realized bodhisattva level, or bhūmi.

The main concern of bodhisattvas is always to help sentient beings, both temporarily and ultimately. This is what differentiates them from śrāvaka practitioners. The relative or temporary benefit is to provide sentient beings with anything they need for their well-being. The ultimate benefit is to support sentient beings to become liberated from saṃsāra. This intention is bodhicitta comprising both relative and absolute bodhicitta. Relative bodhicitta is an attitude of genuine compassion and loving kindness toward sentient beings. Absolute bodhicitta means that this compassion is grounded in wisdom and therefore not sentimental. It is pure, genuine compassion as experienced in a non-dual state of mind; it is not something solid or emotional that makes you depressed during the day and causes insomnia at night! Mind and thoughts are unobstructed and empty, and by knowing the empty nature of mind a bodhisattva supports sentient beings compassionately. Thus, this compassion is not emotionally linked with self-clinging.

The bodhisattva vow

The bodhisattva vow means committing oneself to be a bodhisattva—with any of the above-mentioned three attitudes. In the beginning, when you make up your mind to take the bodhisattva vow, you do so depending on your courage; this is a most powerful moment in your mind. It is the main cause defining what kind of bodhisattva you will be, as you will develop according to what you wished for. Thus, this first wish is very important. You make your choice whether you want to be a shepherd-like bodhisattva, a ferryman-like bodhisattva, or a king-like bodhisattva. You don't have to inform the teacher who is giving the vow about your attitude. Yet keep this in mind as you repeat the words while receiving the vow in both its aspects: (1) the bodhisattva vow of aspiration and (2) the bodhisattva vow for putting this aspiration into practice.

The procedure for taking the vow is that first, from the bottom of your heart, you supplicate to the buddhas and bodhisattvas. Their wisdom is unobstructed, and thus they know when any living being makes supplications. Supplication is your way of cooperation: you make good use of your positive karma by receiving the blessings of buddhas and bodhisattvas. Here you make a very precious commitment—bodhicitta—and receive the bodhisattva vow. For this, you invite the buddhas and bodhisattvas, and they all appear in front of you. They and the teacher who represents and transmits the lineage of the bodhisattva vow to you witness that you take this commitment. Moreover, the celestial beings in the deva realms have some kind of mental power to know what human beings are doing, what precious attitude and commitment you are adopting. The good-minded celestial beings thus rejoice in your merit and support it. Therefore, you invite all of them as supportive friends to activate your bodhicitta. After that, one recites the so-called seven-branch practice, "As many buddhas as there may be in any world . . . [ending in] I dedicate it all to the attainment of buddhahood, the enlightened state." After that, you prostrate three times in front of the buddhas, the bodhisattvas, and the spiritual teacher, and then, kneeling down on your right knee and placing the hands into the respect mudrā, you take the vow. Afterward, taking your regular seat again, the teacher and students make some prayers and wishes, requesting the devas in the celestial realms to rejoice in your merits, as well as making wishes that all sentient beings become bodhisattvas and achieve enlightenment.

The bodhisattva vow means that, step by step, everything you do is for the good of sentient beings, and that you avoid harming them. To pursue this development, you should know the precepts of the bodhisattva vow because this enables you to protect it. The following points are the most important ones:

(1) The main precept of the bodhisattva vow is not to deceive the triple gem of Buddha, Dharma, and Sangha.

(2) Another precept is not to make others regret what doesn't have to be regretted. For example, if someone engages in Theravāda practice, don't say, "This is wrong; you should practice Vajrayāna or Mahāyāna." If someone is practicing the bodhisattvayāna, you shouldn't discourage this person, saying, "This is very difficult; Theravāda is easier." This kind of loose talk, which makes people regret what is not to be regretted, should be avoided.

(3) Moreover, don't talk negatively about others; the worst is to talk badly of bodhisattvas, arhats, and buddhas, because this will break your bodhisattva vow. You don't know who is a genuine bodhisattva or arhat; therefore, it is better to not talk badly about others at all, in particular from a negative motivation such as jealousy.

(4) Not to deceive sentient beings is the fourth precept. It also includes little things, for instance, that in order to kill animals you bait them, to put something there for them to eat so that you can catch and kill them. Of course, it depends on the motivation, on the reasons. If it is for some major benefit, it is different. But to deceive other sentient beings for your own self-interest is a way to spoil your bodhisattva vow.

It is usually said in this context that one can "break the vow", which is not a very precise formulation. The point is that these vows aim at awakening and are therefore very precious and meritorious. Once you have taken these vows, any merit you accumulate will be multiplied because of this motivation. When you commit certain negative actions, this will spoil the precious vows and therefore spoil your merit. To say "spoil the vow" is thus more accurate. The path to enlightenment is your own path, which you yourself travel, and when you make some mistakes that spoil your practice, it is not supportive for your development. This holds true for all kinds of vows, refuge vows, lay persons' vows, and Mahāyāna and Vajrayāna vows. Spoiling the vow means to damage one's own merit. It is not as if you broke a kind of rule. Dharma doesn't have rules like that, that you could break, made by some big boss, person, system, or government.

To restore small damages to your bodhisattva vow, you can recite the *Sūtra of the Thirty-five Buddhas*, confessing and regretting the negative deeds. In case of major negative actions, for example damaging the bodhisattva vow through the force of strong anger, you should retake the bodhisattva vow in order to restore it. Of course, you should not develop the habit of breaking it, restoring it, breaking it, restoring it, and so on.

For details regarding the bodhisattva precepts, you may study, for example, the *Jewel Ornament of Liberation*[31] by Gampopa or the specific section in the *Treasury of Knowledge*[32] by Kongtrul Lodrö Thaye. Moreover, practicing in ways that strengthen your bodhicitta is crucial. Mind is mind. It will turn to the direction in which your attention goes. Therefore, when you think a lot about bodhicitta and concentrate on compassion toward sentient beings, the mind will change into that nature. It is therefore very good to engage in lojong practice, and it is very helpful to read Śāntideva's *Bodhicaryāvatāra*.

Questions regarding the bodhisattva vow and bodhicitta

Q.: I came here to take the bodhisattva vow, but now I hesitate. If I only look at all that I have done in this life, I don't know the consequences. Together with all the things I must have done in previous lives, how can I trust myself?

A.: Of course, you can trust yourself! First of all, you have a good human life; second, you have good faculties so that you can understand everything perfectly, if you pay attention; third, now you are connected to the teachings of the Buddha. And you not only understood about the bodhisattva vow, but you also understand what bodhicitta is, what the benefit of the bodhisattva vow is, and how to develop and preserve it. You have the chance to understand it; the opportunity is there. Therefore, you are full of potential; there is no need to have doubts about yourself. Once you have taken the bodhisattva vow, it doesn't mean that you immediately have to be like a great bodhisattva. You will gradually improve through the various skillful methods.

Q.: Does the wish to be reborn in Dewachen contradict the intention of a shepherd-like bodhisattva?

A.: This intention, to be reborn in Amitābha's pure land, corresponds more to the attitude of a king-like bodhisattva. First you achieve realization, and then you are able to help others. Shepherd-like bodhisattvas wish to stay in saṃsāra. They are ready to face more hardships to be more powerful bodhisattvas. Again, if the shepherd-like bodhisattva becomes a little tired, he or she may also shift to the intention of a king-like bodhisattva. Whatever was already done in terms of benefiting others will never be wasted.

Shiné: the Practice of Calm Abiding, Some More Details

Training the mind and a trained mind are two different things. First, one engages in training the mind and practices shiné. This is different from shiné in the sense of being trained in calm abiding. We may call the latter the phase of "trained shiné".

There are different varieties of shiné practice, but they all serve one purpose, which is to train the mind in a state of calm abiding and then to sustain this state. Shiné is an ordinary state of mind, that is, a dualistic state, not an enlightened one. The attaining of a state of trained shiné therefore does not depend on having the mind purified from negativities, on the accumulation of merit, or on the meditation of lhagthong. For this reason, it does, in fact, not take a long time to achieve the results of shiné. It just depends on how many times a day, and how long and skillfully you practice it. For this, consistency in the practice in calm abiding is essential.

The mind does not exist substantially, or physically. Therefore, once your mind is calm and stable, the resulting pliancy[33] will be beneficial for you in many ways. The level of your training will determine how much freedom of mind you will have to remain focused while thinking or concentrating. When you actually experience this kind of freedom, you are considered well-trained. This is the above-mentioned state of "trained shiné". To get there, you employ the methods of training for shiné, or in Sanskrit, śamatha.

This pliancy of mind is very useful. You may have heard of the so-called "five eyes" or the "five extensive powers" of the mind to know hidden things and so on. You can access these skills after you have accomplished the training in shiné. If you have wings, you can fly anywhere you like. If you are a good swimmer, you can swim in whichever direction you want. It is similar with mental capacities. The mind has limitless skills. It is only a matter of training. When you have trained your mind in calm abiding, you will enjoy much more inner freedom than you do now, and your present, rather limited knowing capacities will become much broader.

Right now, your mind experiences no peace because you did not develop the skills that allow your mind to simply be at peace—in this regard you don't experience inner freedom. The mind is in the habit of thinking constantly; it is like a waterfall and one is totally overwhelmed by thoughts. This habit of thinking is very strong, because the mind connects to everything and everywhere. With incessant thoughts, there is no inner freedom, but constant distraction. If you hear something, the mind connects to the sound. If you see or feel something, your mind is right there. The mind is totally inundated by contacts. There is no rest, no peace. Peace of mind means to be free from uncontrollable thoughts, which means to be free from distractions and confusion. As the mind has no form or substance, there is no limitation to this peace. Thus, calm abiding meditation will result in limitless inner peace, but not more. Awakening, i.e., realizing mind's true nature, requires more. For this to develop, you have to go deeper into the actual nature of mind and thereby overcome mind's ignorance. This practice, however, requires the inner freedom to abide in the peace of mind. On this ground, you proceed with the methods to realize the nature of mind. Through these steps, you will be successful in overcoming your ignorance. Therefore, the focus first lies on training in shiné meditation. As pointed out earlier, it doesn't need to take long to achieve a calm state of mind; however, it does depend on effective methods. It is important to apply various effective methods skillfully. One among the very effective methods to calm the mind is to focus one's attention with the support of the breath.

Breathing and meditation sitting posture

Even though the main causes for the mind's restlessness are ignorance and dualistic attachments, an imbalance in the physical posture and in the breathing can also temporarily disturb the mind.

To maintain a proper balance in the circulation of the breath, you need to know how to breathe gently. When your breathing is proper, it brings about a very balanced circulation within the body. It makes your mind relaxed and clear. The Buddha gave a lot of advice on health, too. One such advice is proper, gentle breathing, which keeps your body very steady and comfortable. This proper breathing depends in turn on your sitting position. Thus, to support the mind in becoming more peaceful, the sitting posture must be appropriate. A wrong sitting posture will lead to physical problems and make your mind nervous. Sit in the shape of a pyramid where all sides of the body are properly balanced. This was exactly how the Buddha sat under the bodhi tree. He sat on a stone seat with some kuśa grass[34] layered on top. Nowadays, we use cushions, and we don't need to go to the forest either. Here are the points for a proper sitting posture:

o The hips should be slightly higher than the knees. If you sit as you would on a sofa with the front higher and the back lower, you cannot meditate. The fully cross-legged posture called the *vajra position* would be excellent. If you cannot sit fully cross-legged, then you can adopt the half-posture with the left leg in and the right leg out. This is called the *bodhisattva position.*

o The right hand is placed on top of the left hand. Both hands rest on the lap or on the ankles.

o The elbows should not be bent but more or less straight. If you have long arms that reach past your lap, you could rest the hands on the feet to give them support.

o The shoulders should be raised up slightly but relaxed.

o The eyes should be open, looking downward and slightly ahead of you, so that you can see the tip of your nose.

o The head or neck is tilted very slightly forward, but not too much.

o The stomach is slightly drawn in while the abdomen rests very slightly forward for balance. Breathe gently down into the abdomen, which makes your sitting position very stable and comfortable.

o The back should be straight. This ensures that your whole posture will be naturally proper, and that the inner circulation of the breath is smooth.

o The mouth is gently closed; breathing should mainly be through the nose.

The three preliminary levels of shiné

(1) Counting the breathing cycles

In the beginning, the actual sequence of concentration should be short. You can repeat short sequences but with breaks in between. Later on, when you are more trained, you can practice for longer periods. With the support of the breath, you focus the mind, maintaining awareness. To be aware means you know what you are doing. Do not try to have extra-long breaths; breathe naturally. Counting the breathing cycles is the first method used because in the beginning it is easier to focus with such a relatively coarse support. The counting is not limited to a certain number to be reached.[35] You may want to support the counting by using a mālā, a counter, or also a clock to set the time, for example, for five minutes.

After a short sequence of focusing on a few cycles of breathing, relax a little, maybe stretch your body, and then start again. It does not matter whether you focus for just three minutes or for five. The point is to meditate with quality. This means to keep focused awareness, without wandering thoughts that you don't notice. Training means to develop new habits. Your old habit is thinking constantly without noticing it—you don't need training in that. It happens all the time anyway. Here, you are training a new habit and, as with any training, it depends on how many times you repeat it with quality. You "accumulate" the quality of focused awareness, which enables you to develop a proper new habit. If, for example, you try to train in shiné meditation for one hour and during this time your mind is just constantly distracted, you are actually just nurturing the common habit of unconscious distraction. To prevent this, concentrate mindfully for just a short while, but with quality. Maintain your clarity, which means that you are fully aware of your state of mind. You are aware of whether you are concentrated or not. Of course, this type of awareness is also a thought, but for the time being this does not matter and is, in fact, required.

What may be beneficial is to additionally visualize the breath as a slightly arched beam of very bright crystal-like light. This will prevent you from falling asleep or feeling drowsy. The visualized light brightens your mind and keeps away dullness. But do not become attached to it. You should not have a vision of crystal as it might be practiced in some crystal cult. The point here is to just focus your mind with the support of your breath. Breathe gently, all the way in. Visualize your breath as an arched beam of light. One end is almost touching the ground, the other end is at the tip of the nose. Don't think this is real; this might cause some irritation. It is just a visualization. As you are breathing in, you imagine that one end of this arched beam of light goes all the way down inside your body, while the other end of the arched beam of light is in the beginning of the nose. You can visualize according to your convenience. As you get more used to it, when you are breathing in, you can imagine that this light goes all the way down to the tip of the toes. Do this very gently, just to enhance your concentration. Likewise, imagine that, when breathing out, the light is almost touching the ground. The light is just a visualization that you attune to your breathing. It is not real. It is not something concrete that comes out of your body and then goes in again, like the tongue of a lizard, going out and in again.

In the beginning, focus your mind with quality while counting five cycles of breathing and repeat these sequences ten times with a short break in between. Ten such short, high-quality phases of concentration with five cycles of breathing are much better than, let's say, ten phases where one tries to remain concentrated during ten cycles of breathing yet is distracted all the while. In the latter case, you are not accumulating the good habit of inner freedom, but the opposite. If you can repeat such high-quality phases of concentration during five breathing cycle sessions ten times, you will be trained very quickly. Soon you will be able to increase the duration to high-quality phases of concentration with ten cycles of breathing and you will be able to repeat these ten times. Many of my students in America can comfortably practice in this way. There is even one member there who in his shiné practice can count a thousand breathing cycles with high-quality concentration. Then the mind is very, very peaceful. For extensive training, practitioners train to have the capacity to count up to many thousands without force. In this practice, force does not work. It needs a natural development, and going through this means that you become fully trained. Once you have gone through this training, you will be able to count many thousand times because the mind is totally peaceful. As there is no distraction by thoughts, the contemplation becomes very deep. The mind becomes used to being totally focused, not in a narrow way, not with tension, but perfectly peaceful, spacious, relaxed, and comfortable. This is not an enlightened state; you can achieve this quality of shiné, or calm abiding, within the framework of an ordinary state of mind. This is the reason why it does not take so long; it does not require the long process of purifying oneself of karma and obscurations.

As you develop your skill in calm abiding, you become able to remain focused while you count, for example, a thousand breathing cycles. You can do so very comfortably because you developed it by counting just five breathing cycles in the beginning. Therefore, start with sequences of five breathing cycles, which you repeat with short breaks in between. Then, as you are eventually able to maintain high-quality concentration during these sequences, extend them to ten, twenty, a hundred, a thousand, etc. Do so comfortably. The mind will be very peaceful and steady. Don't try to have some beautiful vision here or in terms of the arched beam of light. The light visualization should just be a support to help you focus. Later, you won't need to visualize this; you don't have to visualize anyway.

This method tames the mind. The mind becomes very peaceful—you will experience this. Usually, people say that this or that place is "nice and peaceful" because it is pleasant and not noisy. But even if you are at such a place, you may not be peaceful within, not really comfortable. You might live in peaceful and pleasant surroundings, but your mind still continues to be busy and confused.

Training the mind by first counting the breath, and so on, is a very skillful method. The reason is that if you go through these steps of meditation, you will not face the so-called "waterfall experience". Meditators who do not go through these gentle levels, but instead try to get into Mahāmudrā meditation right away, experience almost maddening torrents of thoughts. This can be very challenging. It is a shortcut to tame the mind, but in the process of doing so, you will feel totally confused. It is very difficult to tame the mind in this way. To go through that is very difficult, because you might feel you are going insane. Only very strong-minded practitioners are able to go beyond that level. Less qualified practitioners face the danger of just giving up on meditation because of this. Suddenly, all kinds of thoughts appear, even from the time when one was a baby, which is usually never remembered; one cannot stop thinking at all. The point is that, as the mind is in a process of being tamed, one starts to notice this constantly scattered state of mind, and this is really not comfortable. If a very strong-minded meditator is able to manage, let's say, getting through this one or two or three weeks of maddening thought-experiences, he or she will get beyond that, at which point meditation becomes comfortable. This period is then likened to a river flowing smoothly. Therefore, in order to avoid the above-mentioned challenges, it is recommended to apply the breathing method as taught by the Buddha to train the mind slowly and gently. Then these difficult experiences won't appear.

(2) Following the breath

When focusing the mind by counting the breathing cycles becomes very natural, you shift to the method where you focus by following the breath, which is a subtler method. You can still visualize the breath as white light in order to focus more comfortably if you want, but you don't have to. When you are able to focus very naturally, you don't need to visualize any longer. The mind, having become very peaceful, does not become sleepy anyway. Feeling drowsy in meditation occurs when the mind is exhausted due to its constant distraction. Why should a mind that is spontaneously peaceful become tired? It is very clear and awake, provided you don't eat fatty foods prior to your meditation.

(3) Abiding on the breath

After a while, you shift to abiding on the breath. At that time, you neither visualize the breath as light nor do you follow the breath. You just concentrate while abiding on the breath, and you are fully aware. The mind remains fully aware, right here and now. You don't use any concept, such as counting, visualizing, or following the breath, but just take the breath as a support for your awareness. The mind still needs some support, because it is not totally in a state of meditative absorption. As you aren't following the breath any longer, the two associated thoughts, following out and in, became one. Abiding on the breath implies merely a single thought. Don't hold on to a "one", however; remain gently focused, spacious, and clear. Then you will have profound experiences in your meditation. The mind is very calm and very clear, which also has a soothing effect on the body. From a medical point of view, the micro-organisms in the body become calm, too, and therefore your whole system of body and mind becomes totally stable and absorbed. We don't know exactly what is happening. Maybe these micro-organisms somehow partake in this calm state. In any case, they are pacified, which has the effect that both body and mind feel very light.

Based on this level of calm abiding, or shiné, you can easily practice lhagthong in the sense of Mahāmudrā or Mahā Ati practice because your mind is no longer confused. Due to its stability, there are no more obstructions. In general, as far as meditation is concerned, obstacles may appear. Yet, it is good to know that they occur nowhere else but in one's own mind. Obstacles in meditation always have to do with one's own concepts. Yet, having gone through these levels of calm abiding as described above, you accomplish stable and clear concentration without any inner pressure. On this basis, it is easy to develop Mahāmudrā, which will eliminate ignorance entirely. In this sense, the journey is very relaxed. It is just as Śāntideva says in the aforementioned verse of his *Bodhicaryāvatāra* (VIII.4): "Understanding that deep insight that is fully supported by calm abiding will vanquish all the defilements, you should first seek calm abiding, accomplished by delighting in the freedom from worldly desires."

Usually, Westerners searching for meditation instructions have already tried all kinds of worldly matters and discovered by their own experience that this is not satisfying. Therefore, for most of you it is not difficult to follow this advice by Śāntideva. This is different from the young people in the Himalaya regions, for example. We cannot so easily convince them to practice shiné. A widespread concept among them is that moving to foreign countries will satisfy them. Only once they are there do they discover that this is not the case. Generally speaking, freedom from worldly desires does not mean that you may not have any possessions, and so on. It means that one should not grasp at things, because this is what stirs up the mind.

With these first three steps, you progress from coarse to subtler to very subtle levels of shiné. All three, counting the breath, following the breath, and abiding on the breath, belong to the preliminary levels of shiné.

The three advanced levels of shiné

These preliminary levels of shiné are followed by three even subtler levels.

(4) Understanding the connection of mind and breath

With this method, the meditator abides in the mind by focusing on the connection of mind and breath. When your mind has become calm by means of the three preliminary levels, you will know how to do it. As long as you don't have control over your mind, it is difficult to imagine. This is the first step of advanced shiné.

(5) Applying

Once you have become proficient in that, you will progress to the next level, which is called applying. At this level, you will playfully deepen your capacity of calm abiding in order to extend the skills of the mind.

(6) Perfect purity

This level of shiné meditation is connected to lhagthong, or deep insight. In a more profound way, you will enter into the natural peace of the mind; it is a deeper, or subtler, state of mind.

You will be taught these various levels according to your own progress in meditation. What I have presented to you is for your orientation only. The main thing for now is to start practicing by counting the cycles of breathing. The first three preliminary levels described above are very important. To dance in the water, you must first know how to swim. So start with the counting.

All in all, calm abiding, or shiné, is very important. Without this, you can never meditate properly. How would you be able to meditate with this busy mind? You cannot keep a candle lit in the wind. You cannot ride a wild horse without taming it first. The mind is like a wild horse and therefore needs to be trained with disciplined consistency in practice. The result will be that your mind becomes calm, clear, and energetic.

Diet recommendations

Usually, shiné meditators give the advice not to eat excessively heavy foods after one p.m., which is very true from my own experience. For example, when we do the summer retreat in the monastery for forty-five days, we do not eat after one p.m. During this time, the mind is very clear.

When the Dharma was introduced to Tibet, most Tibetans could not meditate exactly as the highly qualified Indian meditators did at the time when Buddhism was flourishing in India. Many Indian practitioners were doing very well in these early days, but most Tibetans could not follow exactly in their footsteps. They were less successful than the masters of India but still good. Good meditators in India were able to go without food after one p.m., which most of the Tibetan meditators were not able to do. Not eating after one p.m. was difficult for many people, and it was very inconvenient for travelers. Today, the situation is different again. Healthy food is very popular in the West these days, so meditators can eat more nutritious food. It can be very supportive for your meditation to eat more in the morning and only very light food in the afternoon. When the meditation is already advanced, the diet doesn't affect it so much any longer.

Important advice for the practice of shiné

Generally, there is some very important advice in terms of meditation regarding your daily life: Whether it is your job, your family or whatever you are doing—don't be so attached. The main fetter is not that one does what needs to be done, but one's attachment to it. This is what makes your mind tense. If you reduce grasping in your mind, the general Western lifestyle will not be disturbing for meditation.

To conclude, the three following points are the key for successful shiné meditation: (1) maintain a proper sitting position, (2) understand how to focus, in that you maintain self-aware and relaxed concentration, and (3) be disciplined.

You might have heard a lot of shiné teachings. You might have met many different teachers. But did you achieve a calm state of mind? The path should enable you to accomplish the results. For that, it is very important to practice shiné properly, and for that you first have to know how to go about it. In this sense, the information should be intact and complete. Based on this, you have to practice. Don't make the mistake which Atiśa, upon coming to Tibet from India, observed regarding the Tibetans. He remarked that many of them had a tendency similar to someone who loves shopping, always being choosy and wanting to hear something very high, something extraordinary with much energy involved, and miracles. Going here and there to listen to all kinds of things, one fails in being consistent in one's own practice and will therefore not be successful with it.

Questions regarding shiné meditation

Q.: How important is the sitting posture?

A.: The sitting position, in particular sitting straight, is very important. Otherwise, problems will arise with your inner energies. In meditators who lean to the right or to the left, for example, all kinds of emotions may arise, which is not good when you try to cultivate a calm mind. If your sitting posture is not straight but crooked, instead of good results in your meditation, you may strengthen an unbalanced mind, one that is quite sensitive. This might, for example, show itself in that when you see people talking, you might think, "Oh, they are talking about me." A proper meditation posture prevents this unnecessary kind of sensitivity.

Q.: What to do with tensions in the shoulders or in the neck? Should I do prostrations instead or some yoga?

A.: Please check your sitting posture. This is not connected with karma and therefore the remedy usually is not something like prostrations to purify the mind. It is different if someone has the karma of having a crooked body. Generally, neck problems might be caused if you overstretch the spine or bow your head too much. Don't do that. Keep the body in a very natural position. Don't be stiff. Be relaxed, but not too relaxed either. Keep the balance. Sometimes, Theravāda teachers in Thailand teach meditators to sit like this, a bit to the front, lowering the head. I would not suggest this but instead recommend keeping the spine straight and relaxed at the same time. Maybe an experienced meditator can correct your sitting position.

Q.: Can one sit on a chair if one cannot sit on the ground?

A.: To sit on a chair is all right. You should sit straight. Take a harder chair, not a soft one. Only advanced meditators can also sit on a sofa; they can even meditate while sleeping.

Q.: During the course of shiné meditation, I have difficulties relaxing my eyes as there is always some tension.

A.: It might have to do with the concept that the mind and thoughts are identical with the brain, which is quite a common view in the West; you might tend to "think or concentrate from the head". Tibetans, for example, don't have this habit. In their view, thinking occurs in the heart. Either way is just a concept. When you concentrate, try not to raise any pressure in your head. The mind is, in fact, insubstantial and unreal, so just direct your attention to the breath and try to relax. Shiné means that your mind is aware; this self-awareness is not centered in either the brain or the heart. Allow the mind to abide in itself, let your mind be aware of itself, let it know itself.

Q.: It is easier for me to concentrate with my eyes closed. What to do?

A.: In the beginning, this might be all right. However, when you continue to practice shiné with your eyes closed, you might end up developing bad habits that will then persist. Therefore, my advice for shiné meditation is to try to keep the eyes open, looking downward. When you practice on Chenrezig, for example, you may do the visualization with closed eyes.

Q.: You recommended keeping the stomach in and the abdomen a bit out and to breathe down. Sometimes I get a little tense when trying to do this.

A: Breath comfortably, do not try to breathe downward too hard, just lightly. It you try too hard, you might develop the concept that you are not doing it good enough, which causes you to put even more pressure there. This is why it gets tense.

Q.: Do we breathe into the navel or into the space below the navel?

A.: For shiné practice, the advice about pressing the breath slightly down is given so that you are able to keep the posture proper and comfortable. It is not about breathing into the navel or the area below it. In the Vajrayāna, there are other methods where these things are done, but not here.

Q.: I have read many teachings where it is said that it is important to let the breathing flow naturally. But when I do as you explained, I have the impression that I'm controlling my breath.

A.: Here, you allow your breath to naturally become longer; you are not controlling it. You inhale gently and long, and you exhale gently and long. You use the breath as a support to concentrate. You can also visualize it as an arch, a fine crystal-white rainbow in order to enhance your concentration. This makes the mind more relaxed and clearer.

Q.: How should one go about the timing of a meditation session?

A.: It is good to count the breathing. Some people have

difficulties focusing and counting at the same time. In this case you might also set a timer for three minutes or five minutes. In the time between, you may look at the watch occasionally, so it is best to put it where you can see it.

Q.: When I look at the watch while practicing, then I am also distracted.

A.: Don't constantly look at it. You could put a bigger clock in front of you and then look at it once or twice. This is no problem. Don't look at it every second, however.

Q.: I only know the instruction to count twenty-one breathing cycles and then to start again. Is this okay?

A.: Sure, this is very good, provided you focus with quality and take a rest in between. If, however, while counting twenty-one breathing cycles you think about all kinds of things without even noticing it, this would be a bad habit. To slowly develop the capacity to remain focused, concentrate on just five breathing cycles. Then take a rest, after which you again concentrate on five breathing cycles, and so on. With this procedure, you quickly train your mind in the capacity to remain focused and aware. To remain focused during twenty-one breathing cycles in the beginning might be difficult. Therefore, this is not advised in the very beginning. Start with short sequences instead. Breathing meditation is very effective. In fact, it is the quickest way to calm one's mind. The Buddha and his disciples, such as Śāriputra, emphasized this method and did so for good and scientifically proven reasons. The breath circulates in the body. As you breathe gently and at the same time focus the mind on that, your body system, too, becomes pacified. To support this, the physical posture is very important. When the body is kept *straight*, the inner energies can also be *straight*; that is, they can flow unobstructed. This, in turn, supports the mind to be "straight", that is, calm and clear.

Q.: While counting the breathing cycles, the counting is easy; however, at the same time I am distracted.

A.: This is why I recommend that in the beginning you focus your attention for just a short time. The reason for recommending short sequences is to prevent exactly what you are describing. If, to begin with, you focus for just five breathing cycles, it is easier to maintain that concentration. This training is about building up the habit of remaining focused and aware. Concentrate for a short time. Then take a short rest before the mind gets tired. This prevents distraction. Moreover, you can combine the counting of the breathing cycles with the visualization of the arch of light. Do it lightly; don't be stiff. Develop the skill of remaining focused by counting just a few breathing cycles first. This will prevent distraction and drowsiness.

Q.: In my shiné meditation, I quickly get tired.

A.: It may have to do with your physical posture. Please learn it from someone who knows it.

Q.: Is the result of shiné that thoughts get fewer and eventually stop completely?

A.: Thoughts won't stop totally. Shiné will not wipe away all thoughts; it does not resemble the state of a coma. Shiné pertains to a mind in a state of calm abiding. The result of shiné practice is a certain type of freedom in that a truly calm mind has the option to think or not to think.

Q.: When counting the breathing cycles using a mālā, does it have to be in the right or left hand?

A.: This does not matter at all; either is fine. It is different in the case of certain yidam practices; in that context, one pays attention to counting with the left hand.

Q.: As I do shiné meditation practice and my mind relaxes, I get a space-like feeling in which I drift away.

A.: In terms of the shiné practice, it is very important to maintain a self-aware concentration. Don't let your mind drift away.

Q.: In Vajrayāna sādhanās, when the visualization is dissolved and one is supposed to rest in mind's nature, could I, at that point, also practice shiné by focusing on the breath?

A.: These Vajrayāna practices are specific methods. The perfection process, where, for example, you imagine that the yidam Chenrezig dissolves into light and becomes inseparable from your mind, is another type of meditation. If you wish to combine this with shiné meditation with the support of the breath, please add this shiné meditation to your Vajrayāna practice after you complete your particular Vajrayāna sādhanā including the final dedication. In fact, it is very good to do that.

Q.: During this perfection process, my mind starts to wander around. Could I not switch to focusing again by concentrating on the breath or counting the breathing cycles at this time, too?

A.: Please do so after you finish your particular Vajrayāna sādhanā.

Q.: The practice of shiné and of prostrations seems to "re-educate" the mind. Is it possible that one's mind reacts with some strange emotions because of this re-education?

A.: Mind is empty. Therefore, you can learn everything comfortably. If mind wasn't empty, then you would have to first push something out in order to add something new—similar to unpacking and repacking a suitcase. If you consider your mind as a substantial thing, this kind of confusion might arise. Understand that the mind is insubstantial. It is for this reason that you can learn anything you like and that you can change your concepts in any way you like. Please don't be "machine minded". Many Westerners treat the mind like an electrical thing, right? When you are thinking, you think that you are sending some electrical impulses from the brain. This is just a concept you might be used to. The nature of mind is not like that. There is not a kind of energy that is sent out or some kind of energy that the mind absorbs. Mind is unobstructed, very spacious, and very clear. This spaciousness and clarity allow you to know everything. It is very important to understand this.

Q: Can I also focus my attention, for example, on the movement of the stomach or do some other shiné meditation?

A: My advice is that you practice shiné meditation exactly as I explained it earlier. This is how the Buddha instructed Śāriputra and the other disciples, and they were all successful. There may have been many variations added later on, but they are not so reliable. If you wish to engage in meditation in order to achieve enlightenment, you should rely on the teachings given by the Buddha; they are reliable.

Q.: For a while, I tried to focus my mind by counting the breathing or by looking at the sensation of the breath at the tip of the nose. Neither of these techniques worked very well, but I can calm the mind very well when I concentrate on the movements of the belly. I still wonder what is wrong with this technique because when I concentrate on this in-and-out movement of the belly my mind becomes really calm.

A.: In the context of the path toward enlightenment, the concentration on the movement of the belly or on the sensations at the nose is not advisable because in either method you just sense your feeling, which can also become quite artificial. Even if the mind appears to get calmer at the moment, in the long run, this practice will not enable you to enter into a deep kind of concentration. The shiné techniques taught earlier (counting the breathing cycles and so on) positively stimulate the body and train the mind in a way where deep concentration can eventually develop. In the West, some practitioners go to all kinds of teachers, read all kinds of books, and then mix it all together. This creates a lot of confusion regarding Dharma subjects. I recommend you follow the traditions in a proper way. If you mix all kinds of concepts, you will be totally confused by Dharma—this is then an extra confusion, a "Dharma confusion". In general, sentient beings are confused already, and the Dharma is meant to clear away this confusion. Of course, there are varieties in terms of shiné techniques. The point of shiné is to concentrate and to reduce the amount of thoughts. Yet, you should not judge a certain shiné method from the perspective of whether it temporarily makes you feel comfortable or not. A shiné method is considered appropriate based on your experience that eventually it truly brings about freedom of mind as taught above, a completely stable mind on the basis of which you can enter into the practice of deep insight.

Q.: In my meditation, when a certain sensation, feeling, or thought arises, I recognize their nature, let them go, and return to a focused state. Can I continue to do so?

A.: It depends on which type of meditation you practice. What we discussed so far is shiné meditation, the practice of calm abiding. This is different from "mindfulness meditation", which is about awareness. Any thought that arises is dealt with by understanding the nature of the thought, that is, of the mind. In other words, you implement the ultimate view on the thoughts. This view is that the thought has no substantial nature. There are two ways for such exploration. One is analytical. You examine: Does the thought have a color or a shape? Where did the thought come from? Where does it go? Where does it abide? The other is to just abide in the knowing that the thought is insubstantial and unreal, to abide in its true nature, maintaining one's awareness. You should understand that this is a different type of meditation. Right now, we are training the mind in shiné, in concentration meditation. Here, while you are concentrating by counting the breathing cycles, you are aware when a thought arises, and then you do not follow the thought, but immediately return to your focus. That's all. You don't have to apply the ultimate view of the nature of the thoughts; you do not explore them. You don't give special attention to sensations or any experience that occurs. Otherwise, your mind will not learn to remain in concentration. The mind is used to following anything, thoughts, sensations, etc. A mind not trained in calm abiding always follows different concepts and therefore remains busy. In shiné meditation, the training is about focusing the mind and doing so eventually in longer periods. In this way, you will develop the habit of your mind remaining one-pointed. Shiné means maintaining inner peace. The Tibetan term *ne* means "maintain or remain", and *shi* means "peace". It pertains to a state of mind that is peaceful in that it is not perturbed by thoughts. And this is a matter of training. Here, in the practice of calm abiding, thoughts and sensations are all just distractions. It is very important that you understand the different types of meditation and their purpose.

Q.: When I go through the described levels of shiné practice, will there also be these so-called waterfall experiences?

A.: When you develop your shiné practice as instructed by first focusing on the breath for just a few breathing cycles and then gradually extending your capacity for one-pointed concentration, you will not face the difficulties that are compared to a waterfall. When you start your shiné meditation right away by focusing on the mind as such, then you will probably get that waterfall experience, which is a difficult challenge and hard to manage. Only great meditators of the Kagyü lineage in the past have managed to do it.

The Practice of the *Sūtra of the Thirty-five Buddhas*: Purifying the Mind of Karma

Some background to understand the reason and need for purification practice

The pure mind and the dualistic consciousness

Mind's nature is completely pure. Yet, in an ordinary person's mind, this purity is hidden; it is obscured by ignorance, by a "sleeping" consciousness. Therefore, we don't see; we don't realize mind's purity. Instead, we live in a cloud of ignorance. Mind's purity is beyond size, beyond time, beyond anything we can think of. The nature of ignorance also doesn't have size or substance; it is nothing in itself. Thus, as to their nature, the pure and the impure mind are the same. As far as the so-called impure mind is concerned, suppose you separated it from the various types of consciousness that you experience by relating to certain objects—i.e., seeing, hearing, smelling, tasting, touching, thinking, and feeling—then what is left? What remains is the fundamental mind stream, mind-itself.

The ignorant aspect of mind is the dualistic mind. Ignorance means that you are not aware of mind's true nature and therefore perceive everything in a dualistic way. In this dualistic mind, habitual tendencies are formed by emotionally intense states of mind, similar to potent seeds that are planted in a field. These seeds will, depending on specific conditions, be activated and eventually come to ripen. Likewise, when the dualistic mind is activated by various states of consciousness, that is, thoughts and emotions, these habitual tendencies are brought to maturation. In this way, triggered and conditioned by the associated habitual tendencies, anything can appear in the dualistic mind. These are the illusions perceived in consciousness.

The workings of karma

Many thoughts constantly appear in the mind. Among them, there are those which are emotional, which will produce karmic results; we might call them karmic thoughts. All of them arise within your own mind; they come from nobody else. When we look at the three so-called mind poisons, that is, intense desire, anger, and ignorance, these emotional thoughts directly or indirectly produce negative karmic seeds. Ignorance, being similar to a neutral ground, does not directly or immediately create negative karma. It is rather like a state of sleep, a lack of awareness. From ignorance, however, these negative emotions and associated deeds arise. In fact, ignorance and the wrong views that can evolve from it can develop into very serious negative karma.[36] Intense desire and anger are like a carving on stone. These emotions are long-lasting, result in negative deeds right away, and therefore directly cause heavy problems. When the emotions are not that intense and do not persist, they are rather like a drawing on sand, which will soon be wiped out. They create some karma but not as much. When desire and anger are not intense at all, that is, when they are similar to a drawing on water that immediately disappears, they don't last, and they don't create much karma.

The main cause for any intense emotional state of

mind, whether positive or negative, is self-clinging. And any strong emotional state of mind based in this will be "stored" in that "space" of ignorance, just like a seed. With the support of other similar states of mind that connect with it, these karmic seeds ripen. What propels a sentient being into a particular life is caused by such strong karmic seeds. Additionally, many different causes and circumstances interrelate in one's lifetime, which further intensifies certain tendencies that, due to this process, also come to ripen in the course of this particular life.

For example, when the karmic cause for a human life ripens, a human body and a world like ours are experienced. In the course of this life, a person—when seeing an ant— might just think, "There is an ant walking on the table," which is a weak emotional state of mind. Another person in the same situation might think, "I want to kill this ant," which is an intense emotional state of mind. If this person puts the intention into action and deliberately kills the ant, this karmic act is extremely strong. The thought or emotion together with the action have become very solid and therefore will quickly come to ripen into a karmic result. Right now, this ripening process is blocked because this person is still living as a human being in this human world. However, when this life ends, from among the many karmic seeds accumulated throughout life, the strongest seed or impressions in the mind will ripen first and lead to corresponding karmic results.

The process of ripening of karmic seeds in the mind is similar to the process of dreaming while asleep. While sleeping, all sense faculties, that is, all outwardly oriented aspects of consciousness, are withdrawn into the fundamental mind. Therefore, the externally oriented mental activity is reduced. Still, as long as the fundamental mind is clouded by ignorance, other habitual tendencies are accumulating and cause us to dream. The only difference is that these seeds, or causes for dreaming, are not very strong. Therefore, dreams disappear the moment we awake and do not make us experience things in a solid way.

One should understand that our entire illusion of a body and a world is caused by strong habitual tendencies or karmic seeds. For example, you may live for one hundred years in this world—this is a "solid illusion", a "solid dream". Until its cause has come to an end, it will not disappear. Only with death will this solid illusion, which was created by karmic seeds from previous life times, be finished. At that point, you are dead in other people's perception. But to yourself, in your own perception, a new illusion is starting after the one from your previous existence has disappeared. The period of this shift in illusion is called *bardo*, the intermediate state, and it is very confusing. The habitual tendencies from the previous existence still linger on. Yet, day by day or week by week, they fade away, and, as this happens, the strong karmic seeds that are now going to cause your next rebirth come into the forefront. The closer you get to your next rebirth, the very strong karmic seeds for it mature, shaping the illusion you are perceiving. Once ripened, your consciousness experiences this new illusion in the shape of a body and a world environment. It is as if your samsaric mind and the illusion have become one. It is not that your mind is over here, and the illusion as a separate world is over there. You are not separate from your illusion; rather, your dualistic mind is right *in* the illusion. For example, if you are now reborn as a human being, this perception of a human life with its experiences of a seemingly outer world as such *is* the illusion.

As long as the ripening process is not completed, this particular kind of karmic seed that propels you into a human existence can also be disturbed by other karmic seeds. The reason is that until the karmic effect manifests, or, in other words, as long as karmic seeds have not ripened yet, they can be altered by other karmic seeds. Depending on its particular strength, one karmic seed can in this sense also block another karmic seed.

In fact, any thought or emotion that was carried out by a physical or verbal action has a strong impact because the specific mental state was satisfied or completed by the associated action. Thus, by actually carrying out the thought or emotion, the karmic tendency has become a strong karmic seed, regardless of whether the intention and action were positive or negative. Correspondingly, in the ignorant mind, these positive and negative karmic seeds lead to positive and negative illusions. And even when no physical or verbal actions are involved, emotionally intense states of mind alone can already produce strong karmic seeds. This kind of mental karma can be very precarious. The main problem of these entire dynamics of mental states and the associated actions is the huge "space of ignorance" in the mind, which is like a huge TV screen in which all kinds of images are reflected. Likewise, depending on the karmic seeds, any illusion can manifest in the unobstructed mind. As long as mind's true nature is not realized, one is simply overwhelmed by these dualistic states of mind. In short, the unobstructed space of mind is the "space" or "stage" for all the illusions that manifest in, and are clung to, by dualistic consciousness.

It is not easy to understand and see through all the layers of this entire process. Here is one account that can be found in this context from the Buddhist perspective. A long time ago, there lived a yogi in a cave near the river Ganges. He had mastered deep states of shiné; such meditations were practiced in India also in pre-Buddhist times. Through his deep concentration he had attained special mental powers, among other things, the skill to see where somebody will be reborn. It happened that in his meditation he saw how a mother and a child were carried away by the Ganges River, drowned, and were both reborn in a celestial realm. While he was able to see this, he did not see through the layers behind this effect. He had not developed deep insight but simply the sensitivity and sharpened faculties as they unfold through deep concentration. Due to his observation, he therefore drew the conclusion that the river Ganges is holy and purifies beings of their negative karma. Consequently, he told this to others with the effect that, even today, devotees go for ritual washing in the river Ganges, believing in its purifying power. According to this Hindu mythology, the river Ganges is the daughter of Śiva whose abode is Mount Kailash, from where the Ganges originates. This yogi was not able to see the actual karmic cause for the celestial rebirth of this mother and her son. As we saw earlier, according to the Buddha's teaching, these karmic causes have to do with intense states of mind. When the two were carried away by the river, the mother was fully dedicated to saving her son's life, so she sacrificed her life, trying to rescue her child. Likewise, the son was fully dedicated to saving his mother's life, so he sacrificed his life, trying to rescue his mother. In these moments, their self-concerned thinking was not operating, so both were fully and compassionately oriented to help. These intense states of mind and the associated actions were the karmic seeds that at that moment created the karmic causes for a rebirth in a celestial realm: very strong positive states of mind without self-centered interference. Their present lives had come to an end, and no other karmic seeds were involved. The knowing power of the yogi was limited. This is the reason why he did not see through these layers but just witnessed the pleasant rebirth.

Strong mental states are the most active causes in the samsaric mind. Any karmic imprint, even when temporarily blocked in its ripening by other karmic seeds, eventually will manifest as an effect. As long as the mind is clouded in its illusion, karma cannot be wiped away and stopped. For this reason, saṃsāra, rebirth in cyclic existence, continues. Theravāda practitioners fully dedicate their practice toward overcoming the illusion of self-clinging. For arhats who have accomplished the realization of selflessness, as their mind is no longer under the influence of illusion, neither afflictive states of mind nor karmic seeds are operating any longer. Where and how should they, as the lack of a self is realized? As the focus of these Theravāda practitioners lies on liberating themselves from saṃsāra with the realization of selflessness, the purity of mind is accomplished to a certain extent, yet their focus was not on accumulating huge masses of positive karma. This is a difference from bodhisattvas.

Bodhisattvas generate, through the practice of bodhicitta, great amounts of positive karmic seeds. These seeds provide bodhisattvas with many wholesome resources, enabling the bodhisattvas to be of help for others.

There are so many sentient beings suffering in saṃsāra. If there weren't, bodhisattvas would not need to support them. There are, however, and this is why bodhisattvas wish to be supportive. To do so, you need positive karmic seeds, which will bring about positive illusions. Buddha Amitābha, for example, manifested the illusion of the pure land Dewachen (Sanskr.: Sukhāvatī), which appears in the deluded minds of sentient beings. It is not the "real" world of Buddha Amitābha. The cause for Dewachen lies in the accumulation of merit by Buddha Amitābha. His positive potential made an environment possible that certain sentient beings can relate to. From the side of sentient beings, again, a certain amount of positive potential is needed for that. A connection from both sides is required, so to speak.

Thus, bodhisattvas don't just want to cut off their illusion and reach liberation immediately. Rather, they use the illusion of this human life, for accumulating merit, for creating positive potentials, in order to be of help to sentient beings. In this sense, all manifestations of complete and perfect awakening, that is, the nirmāṇakāyas and sambhogakāyas, manifest due to this positive orientation of bodhisattvas. As they take rebirth again and again in samsaric realms, they accumulate positive potential by helping others, which, in the course of realization throughout the realized bodhisattva levels, will manifest in many different forms. For example, suppose I am on the bodhisattva bhūmis (levels); if it is useful for beings, I could emanate many, many, many Shamarpas in different realms and help sentient beings. There is no point in having many Shamarpas in this world, but rather in different realms. Or Nāgārjuna, for example: as a realized bodhisattva he can manifest many Nāgārjunas in many realms at the same time.

This cause, that is, a huge wealth of positive potential, is accumulated by taking rebirth again and again and again and helping sentient beings. When bodhisattvas accomplish realization, they can manifest in these ways. Manifestation does not mean that, for example, a similar body comes out of my present body. Manifestation rather is equivalent to benevolent wishes and their becoming manifest. Bodhisattvas engage in wishing prayers, and what is wished for manifests. I may, for example, make the wish to be of help for fish in the ocean, and this wish manifests in that I take rebirth in the ocean and other fish can feed on me. When bodhisattvas attain the enlightened bhūmis, whatever they wish for will happen.

Śāntideva described that once in southern India or Indonesia a particular yogi made a garuḍa statue, filled it with certain mantras, put it on a pillar, and made wishes that this would avert attacks of venomous snakes. And this is what happened. Wherever this figure was taken, snake bites were reduced. Well, a material figure as such cannot have this kind of effect; the wishes, however, can. Maybe the snakes, due to the wishes of this yogi, actually saw this garuḍa figure as if it were a real bird. As is commonly known, these birds kill snakes; they are their natural enemies. Effects manifest due to interdependent origination.

This story is just an example of how the wishes of bodhisattvas manifest in sentient beings' perceptions. For this to truly happen, the bodhisattvas' wishes require the vast accumulation of merit; it depends on this. It is for this reason that bodhisattvas take rebirth again and again. In these lives, they accumulate limitless merit and become more and more capable of being useful to sentient beings. So positive potential also comes to ripen, just as negative karma.

Another example is an episode in the life of Guru Padmasambhava. When he came to Tibet, the Tibetan ministers who mostly followed the old Tibetan system of shamanism did not want him to stay. Therefore, they slandered him a lot in front of the king, trying to make the king send him away. Guru Rinpoche is reported to have said that he had not yet accomplished everything he had made wishes for in terms of helping the Tibetans but that the Tibetans could not escape their karma. He said that he could have made the wish that the land of Central Tibet be full of trees, but that this was not possible now, given the condition that he was chased away. And, there are hardly any trees in Central Tibet.

In short, karmic causes and effects take place in the framework of one's deluded mind. Generally speaking, through your intense states of mind and your actions— positive and negative ones—you create the illusion of corresponding karmic effects. Moreover, whenever there is some kind of karmic connection with others, what a particular individual does can have an influence on oneself and vice versa. Sometimes, when there is a karmic connection with great bodhisattvas, their wholesome wishes manifest in your perception, bringing about very positive illusions, like a rebirth in Dewachen, for example. It still is an illusion, but a wholesome one that is very supportive for attaining the state of awakening. Sometimes, when there is a karmic connection with extremely evil-minded individuals, their strong negative intentions or wishes regarding others can bring about disastrous negative illusions and cause tremendous suffering for other sentient beings. If you have any karmic connection in this regard, this can also happen to you. For example, if somebody wants to kill others and the targeted persons have a karmic connection from previous lives with this evil-minded person, his bad wish can work out and the persons can be killed by him. The victims' tragic problems, so to speak, were latent negative karmic seeds together with whatever kind of karmic connection they had with the culprit. This is how, for example, Pol Pot killed approximately three million people in Cambodia. Those who did not have such a karmic connection were not killed. Similar examples are found in the recent history of Tibet or China.

It is essential that we purify the mind of its latent negative karmic seeds. The underlying cause for the workings of karmic seeds and their ripening into effects is self-clinging. Given this and the resulting constancy of negative emotions in one's mind, as well as the fact that this has been going on for lifetimes over lifetimes in saṃsāra, one can easily conclude that one must have accumulated a lot of negative karmic seeds. Any of these latent bad karmic seeds, when it comes to ripen, will block the way toward awakening. The ripening of karmic seeds into effects and the illusions triggered thereby cannot disappear until you are fully enlightened, or until you have at least attained the enlightenment of an arhat. It is for this reason that you need an additional support now, a purification practice, so that your development won't be spoiled.

As for the question whether it would be possible to change present karmic effects, the answer is as follows: You can change small things, but not the big ones; those are fixed for the time being. Right now, you are in a human form; you cannot change into a celestial form now. Generally speaking, positive karmic seeds that you accumulate now can counteract negative karmic seeds. For this reason, positive intentions and acts are so important; they are *the* remedy of negative karmic seeds. There are many powerful karmic states of mind; one of them is bodhicitta, the enlightened attitude. Another one is devotion to the buddhas and bodhisattvas. The merit accrued by devotion has the effect that you can absorb the wishes of buddhas and bodhisattvas. It can create a connection so that you can receive their wishes. Buddhas and bodhisattvas made a lot of good wishes for sentient beings. If you have a deep sense of appreciation for their qualities, you create an opportunity for receiving the benefit of their wishes for you. Another powerful thought that can weaken negative karmic seeds is strong motivation, strong regret. Regret is like a therapy to weaken karmic thoughts that are like a carving on stone. This antidote will subdue the power of your negative emotions. Regret does not mean that you blame yourself. It has nothing to do with self-punishment. I emphasize this because those with a Christian background might have this association. Regret in our Buddhist practice is not meant in a self-deprecating, emotional sense. It rather means that you know how destructive your past negative emotions or actions were. You know that their results will also be negative. Therefore, you regret what you've done. A strong mind in this regard is very powerful. These are all relative methods for purifying oneself from karmic seeds. The most powerful method in this regard, however, is the direct experience of the empty nature of karma. This is the most effective method for truly eliminating karmic seeds, but it is difficult. To be able to apply this, you have to develop wisdom.

In the meantime, it is important to practice the relative methods for purifying oneself of negative karmic seeds that you have accumulated in all your many past lives up to now. By virtue of these relative methods, it is possible to weaken the negative karmic seeds within a very short time. At a certain point, you can even eliminate them. But even if you don't manage to eliminate them completely right now, you can still weaken negative karmic seeds to such an extent that they no longer come to ripen. This enables you to continue with your practice and, by doing so, eventually you become enlightened, at which point all karmic seeds have disappeared.

This is how you combine the two methods, i.e. those on the relative and on the absolute level: As long as you are within your own delusion, meaning that negative karmic seeds still continue to ripen, you focus on deliberately creating new, positive karmic seeds by way of wholesome intentions and actions. This will block the chance of bad karmic seeds to ripen, which would spoil your opportunity of further spiritual development. The huge masses of positive intentions, actions, and. the associated impressions planted in your mind weaken your negative karmic seeds and create very positive fruitful karmic results. At the same time, you continue to develop wisdom, which will unfold from within your mind, and eventually your delusion will disappear. This is how, by integrating the absolute level, you will accomplish the state of awakening.

In any case, the strongest method of purification is bodhicitta, and the strongest negative thought is selfishness. A very selfish attitude together, for example, with anger creates very strong karma. If one's self-clinging is less, one's anger is also weaker, and the accumulated karma is weaker as well.

As pointed out earlier, karmic seeds and karmic results happen in the realm of ignorance; once ignorance is gone, karma is gone naturally as well. This is the way it is. It is not made up by Buddhist teachers. This reality is to be understood accurately; this is what one should strive for. This is what the Four Noble Truths are about: describing the truth of suffering, its origin, its cessation, and the path toward awakening. The remedy has to counteract the origin of suffering—and it is for this purpose that instructions on the path are given. The cessation of suffering, enlightenment, will naturally result from the truth of the path. The Four Noble Truths are not something the Buddha or another teacher made up for presenting something interesting to people. It is not an invention, and it is not entertainment.

Questions regarding karma

Q.: Does the system of karma apply to all sentient beings, or does it work only for Buddhists and not for beings with other religions or beliefs?

A.: Karma is not a system. The dynamics of karmic seeds ripening into karmic effects happens in the minds of all sentient beings. Every sentient being has a mind in which many karmic seeds are created, and each karmic seed results in a certain type of illusion. There is no "system of karma" like, let's say, systems of democracy, of communism, of Christianity, Hinduism, or Buddhism, etc. Karma is not an invention by someone and has nothing to do with a judge and punishment; it is something that happens within your own mind.

Q.: Can one say that certain non-Buddhist great saints of the past were bodhisattvas and were free of karma?

A.: That is possible; you don't have to be a Buddhist to be free of karma. Earlier, I used the example of a good fish that offers his flesh to other fish in the ocean. Well, this fish is not a religious Buddhist. Regardless of the religion, it depends on whether one knows what is helpful and what not. The main thing is that you know how to change what is improper and how to purify the mind. The mind of someone who is on the way toward enlightenment is very pure. If you want to call that holy, positive, good, supreme, that is all fine—these are just words. Suppose I had a very bad and hateful attitude toward others, and my karmic seeds propelled me into the rebirth as a ferocious crocodile that devours people and animals alike; what do you want to call that? You may call me a māra or monster or any bad name—that is okay, it is merely language. I am still just a crocodile. If, instead, I had a good attitude toward others, bodhicitta, then I would have accumulated a lot of merit and now become a buddha; that means someone who can help others. That is also possible. Beings can be harmed by other beings, and they can also receive help from others. What do you call that helper? If you want, you can call him a god, a friend, or a doctor, etc. Apart from what you call him, he or she is still the one who is helping you; your label won't change that. This is what bodhisattva or buddha means. It is not something caught in a religious system.

Q.: Can illusions disappear completely, or will some remnant remain in the end, which is just positive?

A.: When you fully realize buddha nature, all delusions will disappear. But that doesn't mean that you are in a coma-like state. There is no need to imagine now what will happen then.

Q.: I find it difficult to judge whether something is a good illusion or a bad illusion.

A.: Right now, you are in a good illusion, because you are in a human form and not intellectually disabled. You are not a spider; that would be an example of a bad illusion. If you have a good human body, but don't improve, don't develop wisdom, then you spoil your good illusion.

About the *Sūtra of the Thirty-five Buddhas*

The *Sūtra of the Thirty-five Buddhas* comprises a twofold method for purification and accumulation. On the one hand, it helps to eliminate negative impressions, negative karmic seeds, so that one's mind is no longer under the influence of negative karma and therefore becomes clearer. As negative imprints become weaker, wisdom gets stronger. On the other hand, this practice helps us to accumulate merit, a condition which is necessary for enlightenment. Merit leads to excellent opportunities for awakening, by virtue of, for example, being reborn in a pure buddha land. To be reborn where buddhas are is the best opportunity for attaining the state of awakening; not only are you born in the area where a buddha is, but you are learning from a buddha, you are guided by a buddha, and you are able to follow the teachings. Generally, the conditions for enlightenment depend on merit, and one should know how to accumulate it.

Why thirty-five buddhas?

The Buddha taught about different universes where there are different buddhas. In terms of the so-called Thirty-five Buddhas, they are said to be in thirty-five realms, which appear to be located relatively close to our world, the one in which Buddha Śākyamuni appeared. Quite close probably means within the Milky Way, that is, the galaxy that contains our Solar System.

Each of these Thirty-five Buddhas has a different color: some are white, some yellow, others blue. The reason is that these colors correspond to the complexion of the humans in the respective worlds. In some worlds, the majority of the human inhabitants have a yellowish color. Therefore, when a buddha manifests his birth in that realm, as a child of a family, he appears in this color too. He then begins to demonstrate his spiritual path starting from the understanding that saṃsāra is problematic by nature until his complete and perfect state of being awakened. Such a buddha is just pretending; actually, he already is a buddha. In fact, he manifests this entire process of spiritual development for the perception of normal human beings in order to show an example of this possible development. Buddha Śākyamuni did that. By appearing as a regular human person, he showed us that we all have the potential to become a buddha, exactly like himself. So he appeared as the child of a wealthy family on this earth. This, too, corresponds to conventional perceptions. Imagine if a poor beggar's son tells you that saṃsāra has no meaning; it might not be so effective. If, on the contrary, a very wealthy man, even a king, tells you that saṃsāra has no meaning, that an ordinary life has no meaning, that there is something else to achieve, it is more convincing, right? People usually think that if you are very rich, you are happy. But the Buddha said, "No. I am a prince here, I have everything here, and it is not satisfactory. There must be something else." So he went to a forest, running away from the family trap. He didn't just sleep in the forest; he meditated there and then demonstrated his enlightenment. All this was an example to his followers: "You can achieve everything that I achieved!"

The Buddhas in these different worlds—which are so fortunate to have Buddhas—are said to manifest in the color or complexion of the particular humans, whether this is black, yellow, white, or any other color. In this way, specific Buddhas attune to the karma associated with certain worlds of human beings. It appears that we have a stronger karmic connection to buddhas who manifest in worlds that are closer to us than those that are more distant. In our present delusion, we perceive this galaxy of the Milky Way to a certain extent. It is visible to us, which means that we have some karmic connection. Even though the Buddhas in these worlds are there and not living on the globe of our earth, this area is still somewhat visible to us in the distance and therefore it is easier for us to receive their blessing. For this reason, Buddha Śākyamuni selected—among the millions of buddhas—these particular Thirty-five Buddhas for us to supplicate to.

What to visualize?

As you recite the *Sūtra of the Thirty-five Buddhas*, you visualize these Thirty-five Buddhas in the space in front of you. Imagine that each is seated on a huge, comfortable lotus seat. One from among these Thirty-five Buddhas is "our"

Buddha Śākyamuni. You can imagine him in the center and all the others around him in any way you like, either arranged in a circle, a square, or a pyramid-like system. When a buddha is teaching his disciples, he sometimes sits in the lotus posture; sometimes he sits on a chair like Maitreya. You can imagine it in either way you like. Having invited all these buddhas in front of you, you supplicate and make prostrations to them.

You can recite the text either in its original Sanskrit version, or in the translation into Tibetan, or in the translation into your own language. When you recite it in Tibetan, you can also read the sūtra in communities with Tibetan lamas, so this might be convenient. In some Tibetan translations, an extra line was added saying *lama la kyab su chi'o* (I take refuge to the lama). You don't need to recite this. It is better to remain with the original text, which does not contain the supplication to the teacher. Chinese Buddhists, for example, often criticize Tibetan Buddhism for its over-emphasis on the supplication to the lama. This is why they started to refer to Tibetan Buddhism as "Lamaism". The reason some Tibetan Buddhists support their emphasis on the supplication to the lama is that, while all arhats and pratyekabuddhas attained their level of enlightenment with Buddha Śākyamuni being the direct cause, buddhas become buddhas by relying on the bodhisattva path and thus directly depend on the bodhisattvas. Therefore, the lamas, that is, the bodhisattvas, are venerated first and then the Buddha. Note that Buddhism was introduced to China five hundred years prior to Tibet, and Chinese Buddhists have a point in warning of the possible danger involved whenever this view becomes extreme and is misused by teachers who—using this logic—put themselves above the Buddha. There is a potential for misuse, even today. I do not want to be too direct and hope that you understand why I recommend you remove this line where the teacher is supplicated to. You certainly should respect and appreciate your teacher when you receive teachings. But here, concentrate on the Buddhas!

The practice of the Sūtra of the Thirty-five Buddhas in the Kagyü tradition

The practice of the *Sūtra of the Thirty-five Buddhas* was done by Marpa, the great translator, when he did prostrations; in terms of Milarepa, it is not mentioned clearly in his life story to whom he made prostrations. Later, Pagmo Drupa, a student of Gampopa, designed or arranged the ngöndro *tsog shing*, i.e., the "field of merit" (commonly known as the "refuge tree") as the objects of refuge one prostrates to. Pagmo Drupa arranged this type of preliminary practice in particular for the practice of Hevajra, which is interrelated with the practices of Vajrayoginī and Chakrasamvara. Here, the assembly of lamas is visualized in the center and the other objects of refuge in other areas around them. In Pagmo Drupa's version, the main lama was Gampopa, who of course, is beyond any doubt. Nowadays, the situation is not the same as in Gampopa's time. A lot has changed, but many still use the arrangement of Gampopa's time as an old rule. This is a precarious subject. The transmission lineage of the practice of the *Sūtra of the Thirty-five Buddhas* as done by Marpa has been fully maintained; this lineage is unbroken, and these Thirty-five Buddhas will never come as human dictators, using religion to control people. That will never happen. Therefore, with this practice, there is no risk involved. The lineage is fully intact; buddhas are buddhas. A buddha will never come as a lama like me or Lama Yangdag or whatever lamas there are nowadays, some good, some maybe not so good. Nowadays, you can be misled by lamas. Therefore, I said that the situation is not like it was in Gampopa's time, and this is the reason why there is a risk in maintaining a system from Gampopa's time. In the Bodhi Path centers, we therefore go back to the time of the great Marpa and do what he did: practicing the preliminaries on the basis of the *Sūtra of the Thirty-five Buddhas*, both the prostrations and the maṇḍala offerings.

For disciples to supplicate to a lama, the lama should be like Milarepa and Gampopa, and the disciple as well has to have the capacity for it. Then such supplication will lead to wisdom. There is a Tibetan saying: "To practice tummo you have to be a human tummo like Milarepa." The meaning of tummo is "very powerful"; it describes a person who never reverses, who always continues, who never changes his mind, who will face any obstacle; this person is like a vajra. To engage in these kinds of Vajrayāna methods requires the powerful capacity to apply a powerful meditation like tummo, which is part of the so-called Six Yogas of Nāropa. Don't be misled by the frequent English translation of "inner heat" for tummo. This just refers to a side-effect of this practice, which is inner warmth; the word as such means "powerful". Be aware that the situation nowadays is not like in Gampopa's time. Nowadays, anybody can advertise himself as a good lama. Anyone can say, "If you supplicate to me you will get a blessing like that of the Buddha, and the tradition will continue." A tradition may continue, but wisdom won't unfold in you as it did in Marpa, Milarepa, and Gampopa. It is for this reason that I recommend the practice of the *Sūtra of the Thirty-five Buddhas*, which is absolutely reliable. Whatever happens, the Thirty-five Buddhas will never change.

In the same vein, I don't want photographs of a human lama in the Bodhi Path centers to be worshipped on the shrine. The 16th Karmapa passed away already, so as a memory and to pay respect to the Karmapa you can have photographs or thangkas of him on the walls. I usually don't recommend any humans to worship photographs of humans. A human worshipping another human is not recommended; it is quite silly! So you may have photos on the wall, but not on the shrine, where you make offerings to them.

People in Tibet and Tibetan Buddhist centers worldwide often follow the Tibetan tradition of placing photographs on the shrine, which can give rise to much irritations. When a person looks at the shrine in a private home, for example, or in a monastery or Dharma center, he will see the photograph of a particular lama there, but not one of another lama. This easily leads to bad feelings and gives rise to politics. What is happening nowadays in this context is very bad. Even if certain lamas themselves do not encourage placing their photographs on the shrine, devotees might do so, and this can become very extreme. Many more things like that can happen. Right now, there are still teachers like me saying, "Do this; don't do that!" But in the future, if it goes on like that, the Dharma in the West could become something very mixed. There is a great risk of a big confusion arising. Therefore, it is very good to maintain a nice system.

The Sūtra of the Thirty-five Buddhas with its three aspects of practice

All in all, the sūtra has three major sections: (1) reciting the names of the Thirty-five Buddhas, supplicating to them and prostrating to them, (2) regretting negative deeds, and (3) rejoicing in wholesome deeds and dedicating the merit to all beings.

This supplication of the Thirty-five Buddhas is a way to become receptive to the benefit of their wishes. In general terms, when one person intends to support another, a certain cooperation on the recipient's side is needed. Likewise, here, cooperation from the practitioners' side is needed so that the Buddhas' support can reach us. To supplicate to these Buddhas with pure devotion is precisely how their good wishes can reach you. You provide the cause to get the benefit from their great wishes. The Thirty-five Buddhas have accomplished the path toward complete and perfect awakening. As they *are* wisdom, all their wishes for benefiting sentient beings will manifest. You *just* have to provide a way for absorbing those wishes: that is devotion to these Buddhas. Here, devotion is a pure state of mind full of confidence and trust in their accomplishments. It means a precise understanding of the wishes, qualities, and wisdom of the Buddhas. It is ignorance that prevents you from seeing the path of Dharma and the result, i.e. buddhahood. A pure attitude of devotion will prevent doubts that originate from your ignorance and invite the wishes and the blessing of the Buddhas to support you in purifying yourself of bad karma.

Provided you take the time for an elaborate practice, you should insert a few steps prior to the actual sūtra recitation. First, you "invite the Buddhas". This invitation starts in the Tibetan text with *tam ché du yang sa shi dag // seg ma la sog mé pa dang //* and ends with *dé shing yang par bül lag na // chi dé war ni shug su söl //.*[37]

In order to accumulate merit, while still sitting, read these inserts, imagining that all the Thirty-five Buddhas come and take their seat on their respective lotus seats that you offered them. Then you mentally create the most precious offerings. Anything precious you can think of—lakes, flowers, etc.—you manifest these offerings from your mind and offer them to the Buddhas like a maṇḍala offering. This is followed by another insert, the sevenfold practice. In the text it starts with *ji nyé su dag chog chü jig ten na //* and ends with *tam ché dag gi jang chub chir ngo'o //.*

Then you proceed with practicing the seven-branch practice: "I prostrate to all the Thirty-five Buddhas, including the countless millions of buddhas who live in all directions. I pay homage to the boundless qualities of the buddhas. I regret all my own negative intentions and actions as well as those of all sentient beings; please give your blessing to purify all this in one single moment. I rejoice in everything wholesome, in the merit of myself and of all sentient beings, including the merit of great beings like arhats, pratyekabuddhas, and bodhisattvas. I request all the buddhas to teach sentient beings. I request all the buddhas to manifest in the perception of sentient beings; don't disappear! I request all the buddhas to liberate all sentient beings. I dedicate all the merit to the benefit of all beings." While you go once through this seven-branch practice, you focus on Buddha Śākyamuni and just think that all other buddhas are also present. They *are* wisdom and compassion, and you have devotion. Thus, due to your request and supplication, they are present!

Another option is that you start directly with the text of the sūtra itself. The first of its three sections describes the practice of supplications and prostrations:

(1) Reciting the names of the Thirty-five Buddhas, suppli-cating to them and prostrating to them.

While still sitting, read this supplication part once while imagining that all the Thirty-five Buddhas come and take their seat on their respective lotus seats that you offer them. Mentally offer the most precious gifts to them. You recite: "I prostrate to the Bhagavan . . ." (Tib.: *jom den dé . . . la chag tsal lo*). First the name of a particular Buddha is given, for example, Dorje'i Nyingpo Rabtu Jompa. Then you say, "I prostrate to you" (Tib.: . . . *la chag tsal lo*). The Tibetan *la* is a grammatical particle, simply meaning "to". It is convenient to memorize the names, because then you can simultaneously make the prostrations with the recita-tion. As long as you do not know the names by heart, you might play an audio recording as you prostrate. You do not need to memorize the rest of the sūtra, because after the prostrations, as explained below, you continue with the recitation of the text while sitting.

Having recited this part of the text once, you stand up and prostrate while you again recite the names of all the Thirty-five Buddhas. When you reach the last one, i.e., *pemé den la rab tu shug pa ri wang gi gyal po la chag tshal lo*, you go back to the beginning, i.e., to *sem chen tam ché tag par sang gyé la kyab su chi'o* . . . and recite again until . . . *pemé den la rab tu shug pa ri wang gi gyal po la chag tshal lo*. This entire section you recite again and again while doing prostrations to all Thirty-five Buddhas.

As you do the prostrations, visualize all sentient beings, including tiny mosquitoes, as being in precious human forms around you. Imagine them all on a boundless plain—it is easier for them to prostrate on flat land. The Thirty-five Buddhas are in space in front of and above you. Everybody can see them and joins in the prostrations. You do prostrations many, many, many times, the long, fully stretched ones. We call them "condensed yoga". These prostrations have very good effects in various ways, also regarding one's health. Among others, they will activate all the beneficial energy-pathways in the body, which serves the unfolding of your wisdom and clears your mind. When you do prostrations with body, speech, and mind and thereby "touch the buddhas' feet", you will get rid of your negative karma accumulated by body, speech, and mind through the three mental poisons of desire, anger, and ignorance. Think that you send all these negativities away as you stretch out, and that you liberate all sentient beings in the six realms as you stand up. This is a way to train your mind and to activate your bodhicitta. When counting, count the prostrations, not the recitation of the buddhas' names. One hundred thousand prostrations are recommended.

I would like to make an additional remark regarding the wording: In the beginning, the text says, . . . *jom den dé* / *de shin sheg pa* / *dra jom pa* / *yang dag par dsog pé* / *sang gyé* / shākya thubpa / la chag tsal lo. This is something like, "I prostrate to, your greatness, your holiness to you, the perfect Buddha, Buddha Śākyamuni." This first long part is not repeated when you supplicate to the other thirty-four Buddhas. Here you just say the name, knowing that this respectful address pertains to them as well. This is how it is usually practiced in the Kagyü, Sakya, and Nyingma traditions. In the Gelugpa tradition, you usually address each of the buddhas with this entire respectful introduction. It might give more emphasis on your devotion, but the buddhas don't mind whether you "address" them properly or not; they don't have a jealousy problem. Of course, you can do it either way you wish; yet, to just use the full version first and then only the names is easier.

(2) Regretting negative deeds

After the prostrations, you take your seat again and fold your hands respectfully. If you wish, you can also kneel down. Then continue to recite the text and read the list of negative actions sentient beings can accumulate. The Tibetan text starts with . . . *de dag la sog pa* . . . until . . . *len ché kyang chö ching dom par gyi lag so.* In the presence of the Thirty-five Buddhas, you regret these negative deeds and promise not to do them again.

You probably have committed these negative actions in this life or in a previous life. Say it with the understanding that these are negative karmic actions and with the motivation to leave all of this behind you; pray to the buddhas to give their blessing to purify all this negative karma, all the karmic seeds that are still in your consciousness.

As pointed out earlier, for something to happen, a karmic connection must be there. In the absence of a karmic link, things cannot happen. Let's have a look at an ancient Buddhist story in this regard from the life of Nāgārjuna who lived some time after Alexander the Great. Nāgārjuna is said to have learned the Greek alchemy to turn stone or metal into gold. Then he gave a lot of gold to beggars, which eventually caused inflation in the country. Therefore, the king sent a messenger to Nāgārjuna, who was told to prostrate to Nāgārjuna and to request him to stop producing and distributing gold. But Nāgārjuna said, "When the beggars come, I can't stop giving. I think now it is time for me to leave this world. But I need a cause to die." Nāgārjuna then tried to identify a possible karmic cause to end his life—having in mind that this was for the good of the country at the present time and would stop the inflation. Through his wisdom he found one karmic seed in his mind that could put him to death: many, many, many, many million years ago when he was a baby, he killed an ant with a blade of grass by cutting off its head. That karmic seed still remained in his mind. So Nāgārjuna told the messenger, "Please cut grass and touch my head with it." The messenger did that, and Nāgārjuna removed his head miraculously. Presenting it to the messenger, he said, "Now I die," and disappeared. I'm telling you this in order to draw your attention to karmic seeds that are latent in the dualistic mind. Nāgārjuna had attained the bodhisattva bhūmis. He was not yet a buddha, so karmic seeds were still present in his mind to a certain extent. However, to him this seed was no trap. He could freely deal with it, like seeing it on a screen.

As you repeat the whole list of negative karmic deeds and regret them, think that they are thereby purified by the blessings of the Thirty-five Buddhas. Don't understand the term *confession* in the Christian sense, but rather according to the Buddhist view. Repeat this section about confession three times.

(3) Rejoicing in wholesome deeds and dedicating the merit to all beings.

The third section starts with . . . *sang gyé chom den dé / dé dag tam che dag la gong su sol* . . . until . . . *dag gi kyang yong su ngo ba gyi'o.* You rejoice in wholesome deeds, and then you make the sincere wish that the good result of your merit, ranging from something as small as giving a biscuit to a dog to the merit you accumulate for the sake of enlightenment, will benefit sentient beings. Make that wish from the bottom of your heart in front of the Thirty-five Buddhas. Repeat this rejoicing and dedication part three times.

The sūtra concludes with wishes for the benefit of sentient beings. This final part starts with . . . *dig pa tam che ni so sor shag so* . . . until . . . *tob par gyur chig* using elements from the seven-branch practice. This part you recite once.

When you have time for many prostrations, repeat the first section, i.e., supplication by reciting the names of the Thirty-five Buddhas and prostrating to them, as many times as you like. Afterward, repeat the second part, i.e., confession, and the third part, i.e. rejoicing and dedicating, each three times. If you don't have much time, recite the first section with the prostrations a few times and the other sections just once.

Thereafter, you retake the bodhisattva vow. This added recitation starts with . . . *ji tar ngön gyi dé sheg kyi* . . . until . . . *rim par shin du lab par gyi.*

After having taken the bodhisattva vow and after you dedicated the merit of having taken the bodhisattva vow, you can imagine that all Thirty-five Buddhas are absorbed into you. Or, another option is that you request them to return to their pure land and to re-appear whenever you ask them to come again. At the very end, dedicate the merit again.

Suppose Buddha Śākyamuni is in Bodh Gaya right now, and you invite him to Germany to teach in the Bodhi Path centers. After he arrives and teaches, you bid farewell to him, and he returns to India. That's the same pattern here. First you invite all the Thirty-five Buddhas to come and stay for a while, and afterward you bid farewell to them. When you invite the Thirty-five Buddhas, they will, in fact, come before you. At present you don't see them with your eyes, just because your mind is clouded by ignorance. Yet the wisdom nirmāṇakāyas are there spontaneously. The moment you supplicate and generate devotion, the Buddhas are present and thus you prostrate and recite the maṇḍala offerings in front of them. Once you have purified your mind of negative karma, you will certainly see the Thirty-five Buddhas. It is true that when you invite them, they really come; and after you bid farewell, they will again disappear from your mind. It is similar to the reflections of the sun and the moon on the surface of a body of water. When your mind becomes pure, then you will really see them. There will also be a chance that your meditation is guided by the buddhas. This is very auspicious! Would you like this? It might be that you have communication not with all the Thirty-five Buddhas, but only with one, with Buddha Śākyamuni, because this world is karmically most closely connected with him. Or maybe you have heard the story of Asaṅga and how he was guided in his practice by Maitreya, or how Nāgārjuna was similarly guided by Manjuśrī.

The Mahāmudrā practitioners in the Kagyü meditation centers in the Himalayas practice prostrations many, many times. Many do not just repeat them for one hundred thousand times but for two hundred, three hundred, four hundred thousand times. They are usually more successful in their ensuing meditation practice. Many of the practitioners in the West have probably completed the fourfold Mahāmudrā ngöndro, i.e., the Four Preliminaries, in the past as well, which is really good.

If you now engage in the recitation of the *Sūtra of the Thirty-five Buddhas* and practice the prostrations in this respect for one hundred thousand times, you will "refuel" whatever you have done before. It will activate all your merit. Therefore, I recommend that you practice prostrations to the Thirty-five Buddhas one hundred thousand times and that thereafter you engage in the maṇḍala offerings to the Thirty-five Buddhas.

As the practice of prostrations enables us to purify our mind of negative karma, it is very helpful on the path toward enlightenment. In addition, prostrations can be very effective in terms of supporting our health. I have even experienced situations where they supported the healing process in case of severe illness. The practice of long, fully stretched-out prostrations is indeed very powerful. I do not know whether it is due to the physical exercise as such or due to the blessing—in any case, they can contribute to the healing processes. It appears that in this regard there is no difference whether one just recites *namo buddhaya, namo dharmaya, namo sanghaya*, i.e., "I pay homage to the Buddha, I pay homage to the Dharma, I pay homage to the Sangha" or whether on recites the *Sūtra of the Thirty-five Buddhas* or the text from the Mahāmudrā ngöndro. It is good to know this. Sickness can happen any time.

Questions regarding the practice of the Sūtra of the Thirty-five Buddhas

Q.: Do we need a *lung* for the practice of the *Sūtra of the Thirty-five Buddhas*?

A.: I gave that lung, that is, the reading transmission, already, and I will give it again. It is not necessary but good to have.

Q.: For a long time, I have had a samaya to say the Mahākala mantra. I didn't do it for several months. Is the practice of the *Sūtra of the Thirty-five Buddhas* a way to purify this failure?

A.: In the Vajrayāna, *samaya* does not mean that you have to do a certain practice or repetition of a mantra forever. It appears that at times it is communicated in this way and that; therefore, many practitioners are quite uninformed about samayas. I am aware of that. You think that when you receive an empowerment you have to do that yidam practice every day, right? This is a small samaya, yes. But if you really receive the empowerment of Mahākala properly, then there are more samayas involved than just that. If you just receive a lung of the Mahākala prayer, then you may do it every day. If you don't do it every day, no problem, you will not break a samaya. In the Vajrayāna, there are fourteen main, eight branch, and forty minor samayas, or commitments. When you receive the empowerment of a particular yidam or dharma protector properly, then you have to keep these commitments. If you receive a lung of the Mahākala prayer or a blessing initiation (Tib.: *jenang*), you have a kind of small samaya, but you don't have to worry that you broke it.

Q.: What is the difference between the "normal" Mahāmudrā preliminaries and the practice of the *Sūtra of the Thirty-five Buddhas* in the sense of its being a preliminary practice?

A.: Generally speaking, the practices have the same effect. However, in terms of the Mahāmudrā preliminaries and the way the supplication to lamas is done in this context, the dharma-political issues of present situations make it difficult and may cause much confusion for practitioners. We do not live in Marpa's, Milarepa's, and Gampopa's time during which there were no problems with lamas. Quite to the contrary to today's circumstances, they were truly enlightened. I recommend imagining the Thirty-five Buddhas instead of the lamas.

Q.: Why is there no Dorje Sempa practice before the maṇḍala offering?

A.: It doesn't matter; you can also practice Dorje Sempa before the maṇḍala practice. Neither way is better than the other; the prostration practice is good enough for purifying, and it is convenient to continue with the *Sūtra of the Thirty-five Buddhas* right after the prostration practice for the maṇḍala offering. You will remember the Thirty-five Buddhas very well if you continue with the maṇḍala after the prostrations. Otherwise, there is no difference.

Q.: At the moment, I'm practicing the maṇḍala offering in the Mahāmudrā ngöndro. Can I start with the practice of the *Sūtra of the Thirty-five Buddhas* after that?

A.: Sure.

Q.: You said that it might be difficult for some to keep the samayas for the Chenrezig yidam practice. Would you advise doing it in retreat?

A.: Once you've taken the samayas, then there is no difference whether you are in retreat or not; you have to keep them forever anyway. The samayas are good; they are not that difficult to keep. You get them right after receiving the empowerment.

Q.: If one gets samayas forever right after an empowerment, then how can one remember them in the next lives? Don't I automatically break them because I don't know that I have them?

A.: Don't worry. If you keep your samayas properly in this life, then in the next lives you will naturally be good. Don't worry about that.

Q.: I don't know anything about these Thirty-five Buddhas, so I have difficulties with this practice. I would like to know more about them.

A.: Earlier, in the context of refuge, I explained about Buddha Śākyamuni, the Buddha in our world. When you know about Buddha Śākyamuni, then you know them all, because the same holds true for all of the Thirty-five Buddhas, just in different worlds. Buddha Śākyamuni encouraged his followers to pray and to prostrate to them to get their blessing because they are not so distant from our world.

Q.: If the Buddha was a bodhisattva and went to the forest to become a buddha, why did it take so long for him to become enlightened?

A.: Earlier I described the shepherd-like bodhisattvas. Their concern is to be in the realms of sentient beings in order to become very powerful buddhas. In his last life, the Buddha, in fact, did not take a long time. His spiritual journey took just six years. Moreover, the enlightenment he manifested after these six years was just a way to show an example. The Buddha showed his followers that, in order to get enlightened, you have to meditate a lot. You cannot meditate while you are enjoying yourselves in a restaurant or bar; you cannot enjoy yourselves in a worldly life and at the same time become enlightened. This is not possible: for enlightenment you have to change your present confused mind totally; for that, you have to meditate. Meditation just for one hour will not change you, so you have to meditate a lot. Therefore, the Buddha gave this example.

Q: What to do when back problems make it difficult to prostrate and if one can do them only very slowly?

A: In this case, you mainly visualize your prostrations and imagine that you are surrounded by many sentient beings who also prostrate. In terms of merit, one prostration with back pain can be equal to a thousand prostrations in a healthy, painless condition.

Q: Is it alright to practice the preliminaries and shiné at the same time, for example, one in the morning, one in the evening?

A: Sure, you can do that. There is no set time for Dharma practice; there isn't any special time. Dharma is merit. Merit needs to be accumulated by the mind. There is no certain time when you should practice. You should do it at times when it is convenient for yourself. The method of shiné meditation is required because your mind is not at peace. For this reason, as you are too distracted by thoughts, you simply cannot engage in Mahāmudrā meditation.

Q.: Can I also do this practice beside the practice I am doing right now?

A: It depends on your development. For beginner practitioners, I taught the method of shiné where one focuses on the breath as a training to pacify their mind. If somebody has already practiced a lot of shiné, of course you are used to that and you don't have to start again with the method of counting the breathing cycles. But if your mind is not calm, it means that you have learned and applied various practices but that you did not implement them in an effective way.

This is why I show you how to start with shiné by counting the breathing cycles. The skill of concentration is very important. When it becomes familiar to you, continue with following the breathing cycles without counting. You need the shiné method to pacify your mind. The practice of the *Sūtra of the Thirty-five Buddhas* combined with prostrations is an additional practice designed for purifying the mind of negative tendencies. It is a very powerful practice and was done by Marpa. I recommend that you focus on this practice of the *Sūtra of the Thirty-five Buddhas* now. Imagine these buddhas in front of you instead of the "refuge tree", the *tsog shing*, which actually translates to "field of accumulation", for practicing the prostrations. This is very powerful. Imagining the "field of accumulation" is good, but I consider the practice of the *Sūtra of the Thirty-five Buddhas* better for you.

When you aim for the Vajrayāna practice of the Six Yogas of Nāropa, one part of the associated preliminaries is the guru yoga in which one visualizes the "field of accumulation" ("refuge tree"). Here, however, I'm teaching you the Kagyü Mahāmudrā practice of Mental Non-Engagement (Sanskr.: *amanasikāra*), and in this context I recommend the practice of the *Sūtra of the Thirty-five Buddhas* for both prostrations and maṇḍala offerings. In fact, the blessing of the practice of the *Sūtra of the Thirty-five Buddhas* is very, very powerful—much better than the practice where you visualize a lama or guru. We are right in the dark age of the so-called Kali Yuga; that means in a time where many things can happen. Therefore, the practice of the *Sūtra of the Thirty-five Buddhas* is very secure, and I consider it an essential part for the systematic program for becoming able to engage in the practice of Mahāmudrā. As I said earlier, in the days of Marpa, Milarepa, Gampopa, the 1st Karmapa Düsum Khyenpa, the 2nd Karmapa Karma Pakshi—when they were practicing guru yoga, their gurus were Gampopa, and so on. There was nothing wrong with these great siddhas; they were almost like the Buddha. At that time, it was very convenient. But what to do nowadays? This security is not there anymore. Many things have happened and can cause a lot of confusion among practitioners. That is what I came across with many lamas, many disciples. Regarding all the various teachers—you may consider them to be bodhisattvas; respect your teachers, but do not supplicate to, visualize, or prostrate to them. Supplicate to the Thirty-five Buddhas and prostrate to them. There will never arise any confusion because they will never do something inappropriate, and you will generate much merit. After you have finished the prostrations, continue with the maṇḍala practice. To those among you who wish to follow a systematic program for Mahāmudrā practice, I recommend to not engage in many different practices. In order to achieve the result more quickly, do not look around for other spiritual paths. Jumping from one method to the next or moving around in circles, you will not truly progress on your spiritual journey. Do not engage in "Dharma shopping". If you do all kinds of Dharma practices, listen to Dharma teachings here and there—this is certainly good for a good rebirth, because you thereby accumulate of lot of the merit. Yet, keeping yourself busy in this way will obstruct your successful practice within one lifetime. If you do ten different practices, you won't succeed in any, though you will accumulate merit.

Q.: If one has already finished the ngöndro and is practicing on a yidam, is it advisable to "return" to the practice of the *Sūtra of the Thirty-five Buddhas* and engage in another round of preliminaries?

A.: That depends on the result. In Austria, some, but not many, have practiced the *Sūtra of the Thirty-five Buddhas*; they did it very strictly, and many of them got the signs exactly as mentioned in the sūtra—so quickly, so fast, because the blessing and everything is so direct. One doesn't have any wrong thoughts about the Buddhas; therefore, the attitude is pure. I have observed another example in Chögyam Trungpa Rinpoche's groups. He taught his disciples to have respect for the spiritual teacher because, through the teacher's instructions, a student can proceed on the path toward enlightenment. However, he always emphasized that, in terms of guru yoga and ngöndro practice, they should relate to Vajradhara as Milarepa! Thus, they are very respectful and grateful to their teacher, Trungpa Rinpoche, despite his having been an alcoholic. But whatever happened, they didn't have any trouble, because their guru yoga was on Milarepa; thus, no problems arise, as Milarepa will not create any problems for them.

Q: What about Chenrezig?

A: Chenrezig is of the same nature as the Thirty-five Buddhas. When you concentrate on them, Chenrezig is included. Concentrate on one practice. The practice of the *Sūtra of the Thirty-five Buddhas* includes everything, all buddhas and bodhisattvas, even the thousand Buddhas of our age. There is a reason why the Thirty-five Buddhas practice was taught as it is. When you prostrate to them, you will receive the blessing from a thousand buddhas, even from one million buddhas—in fact, from countless buddhas! Our common human concepts do not apply here. Many are used to rather think in group concepts. However, Dharma practice is not group-minded, party-minded, or leader-minded. These are ordinary thoughts. Party-minded means you have a group of holy people here and stick with them; this is what I mean by "party-minded". When this occurs in your mind, you have a problem when you shift to another new group. It feels uncomfortable to you. When you are leader-minded, you think: this is my leader. When you apply this concept to your practice, and let's say you pray to ten particular Buddhas, you are suddenly in a conflict, because now there are ten leaders instead of one. These are all our ordinary, worldly thoughts. Leader-mind and party-mind concepts do not apply to Dharma.

The practice of the Thirty-five Buddhas with its three aspects was taught by the Buddha as a method to support the process of awakening. Its lineage is unbroken until today. It is part of the practice of the Mahāmudrā lineage—so do it! And as you practice it, do not bring group-minded worldly matters into it, such as, for example, "I belong to the Kagyüs, Nyingmas, Sakyas, Gelugs, Lama Ole, Le Bost, etc., etc." This is about the path toward awakening. The practice of the *Sūtra of the Thirty-five Buddhas*, in this context, is particularly helpful to purify the mind of negative karmic seeds. This is what you need for your development. This is not about competition between different "brands of Dharma" such as "Suzuki versus Toyota"! What you should be concerned about is to cure your sickness. That should be your target. To cure our sickness, that is, the samsaric states of mind, bad karma, negative emotions, and ignorance—these are the problems we need to deal with, and in order to do so, appropriate methods are required. Therefore, don't be group- or party-minded. And, don't worry about shifting. Buddhism is for enlightenment; buddhas are not jealous. A worldly mind can never apply to the enlightenment path. Everybody should have that clear understanding. Forget the worldly mind in Dharma. The attitude for proceeding toward enlightenment should include first, bodhicitta toward all sentient beings and, second, focusing on awakening by knowing the method and wisdom aspects. The method aspect is the accumulation of merit, and the wisdom aspect is enlightenment that unfolds within your own mind. If you apply a worldly mind to Dharma practice, you will never achieve a good result. Worldly mind means self-clinging, ego. Moreover, there is a lot of discriminating going on in a worldly mind.

Q.: It is said that, in this eon, a thousand and two Buddhas will appear. Are the Thirty-five Buddhas counted among them? Or are they from different realms?

A.: As mentioned earlier, these Thirty-five Buddhas are from different universes. They are not counted among the Thousand and Two Buddhas of this eon. As far as I remember, among the Thirty-five Buddhas, some will also come to this universe but not all of them. These Thirty-five Buddhas are existing buddhas. From among the Thousand and Two Buddhas, only four have already appeared. The rest have not yet appeared; they are presently all somewhere as bodhisattvas. Maitreya, for example, is currently in the heavenly realm of Tuṣita as a bodhisattva and not yet a buddha. The Thirty-five Buddhas are presently existing buddhas in different realms. It is not about past or future buddhas. All Thirty-five Buddhas are from pure realms that do exist now. All of these realms are located near our world; therefore, karmically, they are closely linked to us. If you had a very, very fast rocket, maybe you could go there. It should be within the Milky Way Galaxy.

Q.: As far as I understand, buddhas are beyond time, beyond past, present, and future. Yet there appears to be a difference, in that these presently existing buddhas are somewhat closer to us and therefore more blessing is involved for us. How is this to be understood?

A.: All these buddhas are nirmāṇakāyas. Nirmāṇakāyas manifest in tune with sentient beings; they appear according to their illusions. The state of a buddha as such has no past, present, and future. But for as long as sentient beings are there, these distinctions in terms of time apply, and worlds are experienced by them. So, according to sentient beings, there is time. In our perception there *is* past, present, and future! According to our time, for example, there *was* Buddha Śākyamuni. To be sure, for Buddha Śākyamuni himself, there is no past, present, and future. But according to us, he *was* here. Among the Thousand and Two Buddhas, four such buddhas have already appeared; therefore, nine-hundred and ninety-eight will still appear in the future.

When a sentient being's mind is pure, such nirmāṇakāya buddhas are perceived and guide the being on the path of spiritual development leading to the accomplishment of realized bodhisattva levels. When these are attained, the realized bodhisattva is now also able to perceive the sambhogakāya manifestations. The bodhisattva will be guided by them and finally accomplish the dharmakāya. At this point, nirmāṇakāya and sambhogakāya manifestations are no longer relevant for this particular being, because someone who has accomplished the dharmakāya does not depend on nirmāṇakāya and sambhogakāya buddhas. Rather, this dharmakāya now manifests as nirmāṇakāya and sambhogakāya forms to guide others in turn. So, inseparable from the enlightened mind, these form kayas manifest and support other sentient beings. It is like that. That's the nature of the progressively improving mind. Actually, buddhas are like that. Understand that the state of enlightenment is within your own mind. It does not depend on somebody else. So be happy about your mind, because your mind is able to become fully awakened. In other words, the Thirty-five Buddhas appearing in your mind are actually emanating from your mind. You can relate to nirmāṇakāya and sambhogakāya manifestations due to two causes: one is the wish of a buddha; the other, however, is your own pure mind. When these two are combined, you will be guided by these buddhas.

Q.: Is it possible to make a break of one day or one week while one is practicing the prostrations to the Thirty-five Buddhas?

A.: To interrupt for one day might be alright, in particular, if you have a physical problem. Yet practicing continuously is very good. If you stop for one week, you probably will also not continue in the second week. Continuously practicing the prostrations will positively activate your inner energy pathways and inner energy winds. For that, it is in fact very important to continue consistently. The practice of the prostrations to the Thirty-five Buddhas as well as of Dorje Sempa mainly helps to purify oneself of latent negative karmic seeds; the maṇḍala offerings are mainly for accumulating merit. One needs both, because, on the one hand, purification of karma is required and, on the other hand, the accumulation of merit is needed as well. Don't allow distractions—also in terms of various Dharma issues—to interrupt your practice. When you truly follow the path of Dharma practice, then "Dharma distraction" is also an obstacle.

Q.: As far as purification is concerned, what is the "specialty" of Dorje Sempa practice?

A.: This is also a very powerful practice; it purifies mainly broken samayas, i.e., more subtle negative karma. For example, in the beginning, you may enter your Dharma practice with a strong commitment of bodhicitta. Later on, if you think, "I don't want to be a bodhisattva anymore, but rather harm others," you deliberately destroy the bodhicitta attitude. Something like this will create very strong negative karma. It happens. Dorje Sempa practice is good especially for purifying these kinds of karma.

Guru Yoga with Chenrezig: A Practice in the Tradition of Tangtong Gyalpo

Another accompanying practice that will enhance your shiné meditation is the practice on Chenrezig in the lineage of Tangtong Gyalpo. It is a guru yoga practice. You first visualize Chenrezig on top of your head and supplicate to Chenrezig; you recite the mantra, and you request and receive his blessing. Finally, he dissolves into you. This is a very good practice carrying a lot of blessing, which will ripen your mind. Blessing is needed and, anyway, you have to carry on the shiné practice. Without shiné, you can never develop lhagthong, that is, vipaśyanā, or the meditation of deep insight; and without lhagthong, you will never attain enlightenment. Why? Lhagthong is similar to a laser that can ignite your insight! Please don't take this example literally. I just used it as a metaphor. It is lhagthong which awakens your mind from your ignorance. Therefore, attaining enlightenment depends on lhagthong and lhagthong, in turn, depends on shiné.

For this Chenrezig practice, as you do not visualize yourself as Chenrezig, you do not need an empowerment. All you need is a so-called *gom lung*. It means that someone who has the transmission of the lineage transmits the reading, the wording, to you.

My impression is that many Westerners have some feel-ing of insecurity or feel somewhat empty within. There-fore, many feel the need to pray and refer, for example, to a yidam. For this, the Chenrezig practice is perfect. You can, for example, practice this Chenrezig meditation as often as you like—once a week, or three times a week, or daily—while you are continuing with the practice of prostrations first, followed by the maṇḍala offerings to the Thirty-five Buddhas. No particular amount of repetition is needed for this type of Chenrezig practice. There is no limit; it is very flexible, and will give you a lot of blessing. The Chenrezig practice is also very convenient as a group recitation and practice. You can do all Dharma practice as a group or individually. You don't need a rule when and what to do together, and what not to do together. Dharma is Dharma. Dharma depends on how much you practice—the amount of blessing determines the result you will have.

After you completed your prostrations and the maṇḍala practice, you can concentrate more seriously on the guru yoga of Chenrezig in the Tangtong Gyalpo tradition. At that time, when you emphasize this guru yoga, you should count the mantra one hundred thousand times.

Questions regarding Chenrezig practice

Q.: In this Chenrezig guru yoga, what is the sequence? First the visualization, then mantra recitation, and then letting Chenrezig dissolve into oneself?

A.: You visualize Chenrezig on top of your head. Then you recite the mantra. While reciting the mantra, you concen-trate on the mantra in Chenrezig's heart. If you wish to do so in a more elaborate way, you can imagine the mantra syllables in six colors. You imagine that, from these syllables, light radiates out throughout all six realms and liberates sentient beings. While you focus your mind in this way, you recite the mantra. Afterward, you let Chenrezig dissolve into you and conclude the practice with dedication prayers.

Q.: Seven years ago (1996), you gave the Chenrezig initiation in Austria, and since then I have trained in the yidam practice you gave there. But my shiné is still very poor; shall I continue with it, or should I switch to the Chenrezig guru yoga practice you explained here?

A.: There might be many like you. In your case, as you already started with the elaborate Chenrezig yidam practice, continue with it. However, I recommend that you also practice prostrations, the maṇḍala offerings, and the recitation of Dorje Sempa again—maybe ten thousand repetitions each. Afterward, focus on the elaborate Chenrezig yidam practice again. In the meantime, continue consistently with shiné meditation.

Q.: Do we need an authentic teacher in order to progress on the path?

A.: Yes, spiritual friends or teachers are needed before one is able to relate to a nirmāṇakāya and/or sambhogakāya manifestation of buddhahood. Which teachers or spiritual friends you will meet will depend on your karmic connection; it might be a common spiritual teacher or a bodhisattva teacher. Later on, you will be able to meet a nirmāṇakāya buddha. Depending on the wish of the bodhisattva and your own pure mind, you will meet the right bodhisattva as a spiritual teacher. Or you may come into contact with a pratyekabuddha teacher. During periods where—due to a lack of karmic connections—no historical Buddha is active and where therefore no Dharma teachings are known in a particular world, pratyekabuddhas will appear and indirectly teach people who are able to relate to it in terms of their karma. These teachings will rather be in the form of gestures and signs. These periods of times are called the "dark ages". Right now, we are living in a time in which we are nearing it, but it is not yet the full "dark age". This will be a time when no Buddha and Dharma are known. This will happen in our world in the future and, as said before, during this time, pratyekabuddhas will be there. Due to their wishes in earlier lifetimes, they are able to progress on their own spiritual development even though there is no other spiritual teacher to rely on. Just by, for example, seeing a piece of bone of a dead animal or human, their deep understanding will be spontaneously activated and they realize, "This is about death, death is due to old age, old age is due to birth, birth is due to karmic actions, karma is due to ignorance." Thus, they will understand the twelve links of dependent arising spontaneously. Their mind is very sharp. So, just by such minor conditions, they will realize the nature of things and liberate themselves quickly from cyclic rebirth. This type of practitioner is therefore called a *pratyekabuddha*, a "self-realized buddha". In the life when this happens, they do not have a teacher. In the past, however, they met a buddha and received teachings from him. Based on this, for one hundred kalpas, they have been cultivating their spiritual path in different realms. And then during such times of "dark ages", they are reborn, for example, as human be-ings. In our world, they might be reborn as a European or as an African, as a Chinese, as a Tibetan, as an Indian, etc. It could be anywhere. When, as described before, they lib-erate themselves from ignorance, they start to teach, but not verbally. All this happens according to the karma of the specific people.

This is how sentient beings—provided they have the karmic fortune for it—will have spiritual teachers, wheth-er these are pratyekabuddha teachers, arhat teachers, or bodhisattva teachers. When sentient beings' karmic for-tune is conducive toward enlightenment, they will meet teachers either within the course of a precious human life or within the course of a precious celestial life. Among the god realms, there are also those who are precious in terms of having the capacity for spiritual development. Other be-ings in various celestial existences are not precious in this sense. So precious celestial beings are those who, during their life as a god, meet a spiritual teacher who can sup-port them in their quest for development toward enlight-enment. A celestial existence which is not precious is just a heavenly life without spiritual guidance. If a celestial being has the above-mentioned precious existence, he or she has the karmic fortune to meet either with a pratyeka-buddha teacher, an arhat teacher, or a bodhisattva teach-er. When a practitioner, regardless of whether he or she lives in a human or a celestial world, develops, he or she will become able to relate to nirmāṇakāya manifestations of buddhahood. When he or she accomplishes the realized bodhisattva bhūmi, this person will be able to perceive and relate to the sambhogakāya manifestations of buddha-hood. Someone who progresses through these levels will finally attain the dharmakāya. At that time, a teacher is no longer required; this is the complete and perfect state of a buddha. It is very exciting.

Among these different celestial realms, there are those called the "formless realms". Beings in these formless realms are not fortunate regarding further development. These types of existence are merely the outcome of karmic actions of deep meditative absorption and will last for a long time but will finally come to an end again. Afterward, because there was no guidance toward enlightenment, these beings will continue to be reborn in cyclic existence. Then there are those celestial types of beings referred to as those of the form realms, with seventeen subdivisions.[38] Many of these celestial beings have the good fortune to meet a buddha and other spiritual teachers. Finally, there are the celestial beings within the desire realm, to which human life also belongs. Many of these celestial beings are very fortunate in that they have met either Buddha Śākyamuni, pratyekabuddhas, arhats, or bodhisattva teachers and proceed on their path toward enlightenment. Within the desire realm, there is also another type of existence called asuras or demi-gods. Even though they can meet buddhas and bodhisattvas, most of the time they are involved in conflicts and therefore do not look for a spiritual teacher.

As far as teachers are concerned, both in Tibetan society and in Western Buddhist society, there have been many problems. When you receive teachings from a particular spiritual teacher, you should relate to this person with respect. This teacher is part of the Sangha of those who guide others on the Buddhist path. However, you do not have to worship the teachers. In Tibetan society, having been acquainted with Buddhism for hundreds of years, and, knowing their own culture and workings in society, they know this. The Tibetans are well-informed. Western-ers usually do not understand the Tibetan culture and their political situation very well. They often think that all that is done in this society is religious when, in fact, religion and politics are all mixed up, which leads to a lot of confu-sion in the Western community of Tibetan Buddhists.

Just follow the Buddha's teachings as they are eluci-dated in the sūtras and tantras. Abide by the content of these writings. Genuine teachers will give explanations that are exactly in accordance with these teachings. Apply them. When it comes to real empowerments, I always rec-ommend old, reliable lamas to give empowerments. Then these are genuine. Nowadays, I usually don't recommend young rinpoches or lamas, to give empowerments. It is too early. It is better if empowerments are bestowed by mature teachers, when they become older, sixty-five years or so, have done many retreats and are a rinpoche, like Lama Gendün Rinpoche. He was not a tulku, a recognized re-incarnation, but has been in meditation continuously for many years. Lamas like that kind are very reliable. When you really receive an empowerment from that kind of lama, you can think that the lama and the yidam are insepara-ble, as taught in Vajrayāna practice. Yet, nowadays, this is very rare. As far as the ritual is concerned, actually anyone could perform an empowerment. You just study the text on how to do it and then do it. You could do that; I could teach you how to do it. Everyone can do this. It is very easy: you just follow the text and use the ritual objects! Su-perficially, it is very easy. But to give a real empowerment through meditation is very difficult. One has to be really qualified for that. Empowerment means to activate the dharmakāya, sambhogakāya, and nirmāṇakāya, which are inherent in your mind. When I give an empowerment of body, speech, and mind to you, I have to activate the dharmakāya, sambhogakāya, and nirmāṇakāya in you. I must have the spiritual power to do so, and this is very difficult. As a student, you usually do not have the capacity to see who has the power to do so and who doesn't, which is quite a dilemma and can be very confusing. As mentioned earlier, anybody can read the text and place the vase on your head. In Bodhi Path centers, only those lamas who have at least some power in this regard and are therefore capable to actually give the initiations will be requested to give empowerments.

Now you received the lung for the prayer to, and the mantra of, Buddha Śākyamuni from me by listening. You should always recite it. It carries a lot of blessing. Whatever practice you do, I recommend that you always recite *teyata om muni muni mahā muni śākya muni yé soha* beforehand. It will make your practice very successful. You will not be disturbed by any obstacles, triggered either by one's own bad karma or by evil beings that harm practitioners. These things can happen, but this *dhāraṇī* prevents it. I wrote a *Sādhanā of Śākyamuni Buddha*[39] about twenty years ago. It was also translated into English. We received a copy of my own text from one of Kalu Rinpoche's centers in America—they are still doing that practice. In the Bodhi Path centers, you can engage in this practice of Buddha Śākyamuni, as well as of Buddha Amitābha, of Chenrezig, and of Green Tārā.

Q.: I would like to do a retreat in a Bodhi Path center for one week. What practice would you advise?

A.: If you do a retreat individually, follow the systematic Bodhi Path program. As a beginner, practice shiné to train your mind. Along with that, practice prostrations to the Thirty-five Buddhas. It is very good to do the prostrations in the morning and to practice shiné during the rest of the day. In addition, you can also practice the Chenrezig guru yoga meditation in the tradition of Tangtong Gyalpo in the afternoons or evenings.

An Outlook: Where the Practice is Heading for Including the Uncommon Mahāyāna Path

If you are very successful with following this Bodhi Path program, you will achieve the path of seeing,[40] which means that you will directly perceive the truth. You will not be fully enlightened like the Buddha, but you will be beyond saṃsāra. At this point, you will be a realized bodhisattva. Moreover, this liberation will not just benefit yourself but also others. If you don't achieve the path of seeing in this life, then spontaneously and naturally you will achieve it in the next life or in the life after the next. Ongoing, you will make maximum progress.

In the Vajrayāna, there are many yidam practices, such Chakrasamvara, Vajrayoginī, Hevajra, Kālachakra, etc.; any practice that you do is about achieving the path of seeing. Which yidam to choose depends on which yidam you are connected with. The choice of a yidam for your practice therefore depends on the predictions of the yidam or of the lama. Nowadays, the majority of humans in this world seem to be very much connected to Chenrezig; so, according to my predictions, Chenrezig is the most suitable yidam for most people. As your karmic connection is predominantly with Chenrezig, I selected Chenrezig as the yidam for everybody.

In the different levels of Tantra—Kriyātantra, Upatantra, Yogatantra, Mahā, Anu and Atiyogatantra[41]—there are many different forms of Chenrezig practice. Here at Bodhi Path, you will practice Chenrezig as guru yoga first; later you can practice Chenrezig as a yidam of the hightest tantra. In this highest tantra class, there are two, the red Chenrezig and the white Chenrezig. I selected the white Chenrezig. This lineage came from all four schools of Buddhism in Tibet. The lineage of the white Chenrezig of the hightest tantra goes back to many different siddhas and was implemented in Tibet by King Songtsen Gampo. Later, other new lineages came from India, and finally all were united into one. This version is preserved in the *Rinchen Terdzö*, the *Precious Treasury of Termas*,[42] which is passed down within the Nyingma lineage, although it is not necessarily only a Nyingma practice. It was preserved in this collection of termas in order to prevent its disappearance.

The four empowerments, or *abhiṣekas*, of the white Chenrezig will be given to you according to the *Rinchen Terdzö*; the *jenang* (blessing empowerment) will be given to you following the *Chigshe Kündröl*, a collection of initiations called *One Realized, All Accomplished*,[43] which was compiled by the 9th Karmapa. You require such empowerments for the generation process of the corresponding practices on Chenrezig. The generation process is practiced in order to eliminate samsaric birth, life, death, and bardo. The structure of the generation process is arranged in order to purify the tendencies of these four phases. The generation process will then be combined with the perfection process, which has two aspects, a general one and a particular one. The latter is the perfection process which combines Mahāmudrā and Mahā Ati and will be given as a separate instruction, or *tri*,[44] as it is called in Tibetan. The one that we will use in this regard is called *The Union of Mahāmudrā and Mahā Ati*,[45] which was vastly spread by Karma Chagme. We will teach you that so that you can study this text and meditate accordingly.

All Vajrayāna practices involve generation and perfection processes. The generation process consists of the methods that support the practitioner in a way that he or she can actually practice the perfection process. The latter consists mainly in prajñāpāramitā meditation and therefore comprises the direct path to enlightenment. In short, the practice of the perfection process supported by the generation process is the Vajrayāna. The practice of the perfection process without the generation process is the Sūtrayāna. Usually, the combination of the generation and perfection process is faster and more effective. But in order to practice this, you have to protect it very well by virtue of the Vajrayāna precepts, the samayas.

For the generation process, the associated empowerments are required. Once you have received the empowerment, you have to strictly keep your samayas in order not to spoil the practice of your generation process. For that, you have to know the samayas, and you have to know how to protect your practice. There are lists of things to be aware of so that you do not make mistakes that can spoil your practice.

If you don't have the courage to go through the strict practice of the generation process, you can also practice the perfection process only, without the support of the generation process. It takes a little bit longer and is without any empowerment. If you don't want to keep the strict precepts of the Vajrayāna, you don't have to receive the empowerment. In this case, you continue with the short Chenrezig guru yoga practice in the tradition of Tangtong Gyalpo and meditate directly according to the perfection process. This is also possible.

The Bodhi Path program provides both: an elaborate version of Chenrezig practice involving the generation process and the strict Vajrayāna precepts going along with it, and the Chenrezig guru yoga practice in the tradition of Tangtong Gyalpo without the need of an empowerment and the associated samayas.

In any case, before you get there, you have to go through the preliminary practice. Moreover, you take the bodhisattva vow, where you make the strong commitment to be a genuine bodhisattva for sentient beings. As I told you, there are three kinds of bodhisattvas—shepherd-like bodhisattvas, ferryman-like bodhisattvas, and king-like bodhisattvas. You make the strong commitment to develop into one of them. Then learn how to be a bodhisattva by reading Śāntideva's *Bodhicaryāvatāra*. Based on these studies, you will know how to be a relaxed and happy-minded bodhisattva.

Moreover, the practice of prostrations is very, very important—so do them by all means. They purify the negative karma that you have naturally accumulated through actions. Whatever sentient beings do is influenced by the three mental poisons of desire, anger, and ignorance so that they naturally accumulate karma boundlessly. When certain karmic seeds ripen, your opportunity for further spiritual development could be blocked. So it is very important to use strong methods to weaken your negative karma or to eliminate it altogether. For instance, one of the most powerful negative karmic deeds is to kill one's parents. In your past lives, you may have done something like that. Okay, when one kills one's parents one usually goes straight to the lower realms without postponement. The result will happen immediately after this life has ended; such karma is the most powerful type. But very intense negative karmic seeds due to some similar actions can still be stored in your mind. Once they ripen, your precious opportunity will be spoiled.

It is very important to rely on very effective methods to weaken all the negative karmic seeds in order for you to have this golden opportunity ongoing, life after life. I therefore strongly recommend the prostrations to the Thirty-five Buddhas as a method for purification. The other recommendation is the practice of maṇḍala offerings because by doing so you create tremendous positive tendencies. If you have many things to give to sentient beings now, that is also good. If you don't, you can mentally train to give away, give away, give away. You can say this is a kind of powerful "mental therapy of generating a meritorious mind", to be without attachment to anything. That is very good. Mentally, when you train your mind in giving, that is very powerful merit; it will really happen later! Realized bodhisattvas on the bhūmis are capable of emanating very rich and comfortable universes for sentient beings to be born there. The cause for that comes from this kind of training of your mind, that nothing is for yourself, that you always give away, give away, give away. The maṇḍala practice was designed for that. There are two recipients of offerings: on the one hand, the suffering sentient beings; on the other hand, holy beings. Both offerings collect merit power. For sentient beings, you have to have a certain samādhi power to manifest in the form of Chenrezig and emanate things for sentient beings, like suitable food for ghosts and hungry ghosts. However, to do that you need to have attained a certain power; so to be able to give real things in this way is a long process. Until then you can collect merit though general generosity, but it won't be truly powerful merit. Therefore, practice the maṇḍala offerings to the Thirty-five Buddhas first; this will collect merit power. If you make offerings to these buddhas, they don't have to actually receive your offerings. The wish of these Buddhas is already there; therefore, if you generate thoughts of offerings to the Thirty-five Buddhas, you are already collecting merit. It doesn't depend on these Buddhas actually receiving your offerings! Offerings to beings in the lower realms have to be seen and actually received by them. So there is this slight difference; therefore, I first recommend the practice of the maṇḍala offerings.

If you have already done the Four Preliminaries with the visualization of the "refuge tree", you can do about ten thousand prostrations to the Thirty-five Buddhas, and about ten thousand repetitions of the maṇḍala offerings to the Thirty-five Buddhas. You don't need to start the recitation of Dorje Sempa again if you have already done it. Don't abandon it completely; keep on doing some, to "refill". Repeat these preliminary practices from time to time.

Even if you have already received the short Chenrezig

empowerment, in the future, in case you start with the main practice of the generation and perfection processes of Chenrezig, you should receive the associated empowerment again. As explained earlier, this type of perfection process is the Mahāmudrā practice based on the generation process. At the time when you start with the elaborate Chenrezig practice, you receive more detailed teachings on the perfection process, i.e., Mahāmudrā and Mahā Ati teachings; according to the progress of the individual practitioner, these teachings will be given in more and more detail.

The ground for being able to proceed in this way in the future is the shiné meditation as was taught. You have to do it, because without shiné you will never be able to practice lhagthong properly, and without lhagthong you will never be able to practice the perfection process, i.e., the Mahāmudrā level of lhagthong. Lhagthong is the deep view that eliminates all ignorance. By engaging in the practice of lhagthong, your ignorance is cleared away and, simultaneously, your wisdom unfolds. But without shiné you will never be able to do it; you will not be able to use the lhagthong view with respect to your ignorance. Therefore, you must put an effort into first attaining the result of shiné.

Part II
The Bodhi Path Curriculum:
Meditation and Studies, a Summary[46]

Bodhi Path offers a curriculum for meditation practice and study that is rooted in authentic Dharma teachings and is suited to the needs and conditions of modern-day dharma practitioners.

The Bodhi Path curriculum is based on the teachings of mind training (Tib.: *lojong*), a profound system of contemplative practices that helps bring mindfulness, awareness, and insight to our experiences, both on and off the meditation cushion. These teachings have been preserved by an unbroken lineage of masters since the time of the Buddha and are presented at all Bodhi Path centers, along with supporting practices and study topics, according to an approach compiled by the 14th Shamarpa, Mipham Chökyi Lodrö.

The primary text for the Bodhi Path curriculum is the 14th Shamarpa's *The Path to Awakening: A Commentary on Je Chekawa Yeshé Dorjé's Seven Points of Mind Training*, which serves as a guidebook to the stages of mind training. These lojong teachings follow in the tradition of Gampopa, who joined the Kadampa instructions of Atiśa with Mahāmudrā teachings from the tradition of the great Indian Mahāsiddha Saraha. This oral transmission is known as the "Confluence of the Two Streams of Mahāmudrā and Kadam" (*bka' phyag chu bo gnyis 'dres*).

The curriculum is taught at Bodhi Path centers and should be undertaken with the guidance of a qualified teacher.

Curriculum for Meditation

Core practices

The core system of practice for Bodhi Path centers is the Seven Points of Mind Training (Tib.: *lojong*). The foundation of mind training is calm abiding meditation (Tib.: *shiné*, Sanskr.: *śamatha*), which helps develop mental peace, stability, and focus. With a calm mind comes the ability to practice insight meditation (Tib.: *lhagthong*, Sanskr.: *vipaśyanā*), which involves an analysis of mind's true nature.

Through these practices of calm abiding and insight, we can remove the veils of ignorance and confusion, which prevent us from experiencing the peace and clarity that is already present within our minds.

Additional practices

In addition to the core practices of calm abiding and insight meditation, the Bodhi Path centers teach additional contemplative practices that help support our path of training the mind. These practices help us purify negative actions, habitual veils, and karmic obscurations; accumulate merit; develop compassion; and dedicate the merits of our positive actions for the benefit of all beings:

- Thirty-five Buddhas
- Chenrezig (*Avalokiteśvara*) in the tradition of Tangtong Gyalpo
- Dorje Sempa (*Vajrasattva*)
- Practice of the Bodhisattva Wish, according to the commentary on the *Wishing Prayer of the Ārya Samantabhadra*

These practices require explanation and instruction by a qualified teacher and are taught at regular intervals at most Bodhi Path centers. They are typically undertaken by the practitioner as a personal practice.

Practices to be specially chosen for individuals according to their qualities and aptitudes, with the help of the root master

- Practice of Avalokiteśvara (the advanced type of Chenrezig practice)
- Practice of Buddha Amitābha (requires lineage transmission and empowerment)
- Karma Kagyü Mahāmudrā practice (lineage practice)
- Kagyü Mahāmudrā (the stages of practice in relation to the blessing received from the short supplication to Vajradhara and the lineage holders; lineage practice)
- Highest Practice for Enlightenment (lineage practice)

Curriculum for Study

Studies regarding Buddhist meditation

With meditation, we train our minds to rest in a calm and clear state. Based on this, we are able to realize mind's peaceful nature and innate wisdom. The primary guidebook for meditation at Bodhi Path centers is *The Path to Awakening,* a commentary on the Seven Points of Mind Training (Tib.: *lojong*), by the 14th Shamarpa, Mipham Chökyi Lodrö. At the Bodhi Path centers, the study of meditation emphasizes the following topics:

Preliminaries

- The four thoughts that turn the mind toward enlightenment: precious human existence, impermanence, karma, and the defects of samsara
- Refuge and the qualities of the Three Jewels of Buddha, Dharma, and Sangha: according to *The Bringing the Qualities of the Three Jewels to Mind Sūtra* and the *sūtra* commentary by *Tāranātha*
- Training in the practice of calm abiding meditation (Tib.: *shiné,* Sanskr.: *śamatha*): according to *The Path to Awakening*

Absolute and relative bodhicitta (the wisdom and compassion aspects of enlightened mind)

- Training in the practices of insight meditation (Tib.: *lhaktong,* Sanskr.: *vipaśyanā*): meditation on the unborn nature of mind, according to *The Path to Awakening*

- Training in the meditation of giving and taking (Tib.: *tonglen*): the union of relative and absolute bodhicitta, according to *The Path to Awakening*

Additional points of mind training

- Converting adversities into the path of awakening
- Training in fully integrating mind training in one's life
- The measure of mind training
- Commitments of mind training
- Advice for mind training

Studies regarding Buddhist conduct and ethics

Buddhist conduct and ethics, grounded in mindfulness, form the basis of the path to awakening. They provide guidance in understanding which of our motives and actions are conducive to development on the path and which are not. The Bodhi Path centers teach conduct and ethics based on certain chapters of *The Jewel Ornament of Liberation* by Gampopa, emphasizing the following topics:

Chapter 1: Buddha nature; understanding our birthright, the potential to awaken to the inherently enlightened nature of our mind

Chapter 2: The working basis for the spiritual path; understanding the precious human existence which allows us to engage on the spiritual path to awakening

Chapter 3: The conditions required for spiritual progress; understanding the importance of the spiritual guide

Chapter 6: Karma and its result; understanding the ten virtuous and non-virtuous actions

Chapters 9–11: Bodhicitta and the bodhisattva vow

Chapters 12–17: The six transcendent qualities (Sanskr.: *pāramitās*); exploring the qualities of generosity, ethical conduct, patience, enthusiastic effort, meditative concentration, and wisdom

Chapters 20–21: Buddhahood, the awakened state; understanding buddhahood as fruition, the state of awakening, and exploring a buddha's scope of action

Studies regarding the Buddhist view of reality

In order to develop our meditation practice, it is helpful to study the Buddhist view of reality. By studying and understanding the nature of phenomena and our experiences, we can begin to unlock the vast wealth of wisdom already present within us, understand the workings of mind in our day-to-day lives, and develop a profound meditation practice that can lead to realization.

The following topics from the Abhidharma, based on the text *The Gateway to Knowledge*[47] by Mipham Rinpoche, inspire us and point the way to developing a mind free from confusion:

- The five aggregates (Sanskr.: *skandha*); form, and the various functions of consciousness which comprise the bases upon which self-clinging perpetuates itself
- The fifty-one mental events; an in-depth look at the fourth aggregate, formations
- The eighteen mental seeds; how the senses—our perception of and interaction with the world—and the

various workings of consciousness lead to a continuity of lives in the cycle of rebirths

- The twelve sense sources; the ways in which the senses and perception arise and develop (with the support of the Sautrāntika philosophy)
- The twelve links of interdependence; how ignorance inevitably triggers the chain of events that perpetuates samsaric existence, seen from the perspective of the Madhyamaka (middle way) philosophy
- Karma and the explanation of the six causes and four conditions
- The four noble truths (in detail); saṃsāra in terms of its causes (origin) and effects (suffering), and nirvana with its causes (the path) and effect (the fruition of cessation)
- The twenty-two faculties; the phenomenological faculties that determine our experience of life
- The three yānas and the five paths; the three vehicles or approaches to Buddhist practice and their definition of progressive spiritual development
- The conditioned and the non-conditioned; that which is conditioned, in that it arises and ceases based on causes and conditions, and that which is not
- Time and its workings
- Relative and absolute truth (according to *The Ornament of Madhyamaka* by Śāntarakṣita[48])

Studies of additional subjects

- Perception; direct, accurate perception and inferential accurate perception (i.e. the Buddhist theory of knowledge, mind, and its workings)

- The states of meditative concentration; the ground as to the progressive states of meditative absorption, according to chapter eight of Vasubandhu's *Abhidharmakośa,* i.e., *The Compendium of Higher Knowledge of Phenomena*[49]
- Wisdom; fruition as primordial awareness, the insight of wisdom, emerging as the fruition, according to chapter seven of Vasubandhu's *Abhidharmakośa,* i.e., *The Compendium of Higher Knowledge of Phenomena*

Endnotes

1 Tib. transliteration: *na ro chos drug*; Tib. phonetics: *naro chödrug*. These six particular types of practice are part of the so-called perfection process of tantric meditation. They are: (1) the powerful one (often translated as "inner heat"), (2) illusory body, (3) dream, (4) luminosity, (5) intermediate state, and (6) transference. In the same sequence, the Tibetan transliteration is: *gtum mo, sgyu lus, rmi lam, 'od gsal, bar do*, and *'pho ba*. Tib. phonetics: *tummo, gyulü, milam, ösal, bardo*, and *powa*.

2 The Mahāsiddhas Nāropa (1016–1100) and Tilopa (988–1069) were two of the most important Indian sources for Tibetan Dagpo Mahāmudrā; Marpa (Tib. transliteration: Mar pa, approx. 1012–1097), a famous translator, was the first Tibetan lineage holder. His disciple Milarepa (Tib. transliteration: Mi la ras pa, 1040–1123) is considered the most famous yogi in Tibet and is said to have attained enlightenment in one lifetime. His most important student was Gampopa (Tib. transliteration: Sgam po pa, 1079–1153), also called Dagpo Lharje, the healer from Dagpo, an area in the south of Tibet. The tradition is therefore called Dagpo Kagyü (Tib. transliteration: Dwags po Bka' brgyud).

3   All of these masters are most important sources for Tibetan Dagpo Mahāmudrā. Regarding Saraha, there is no certainty about his dates. Modern historians place him around the ninth century CE. Traditional Tibetan sources place him in a range of several hundred years, anywhere from two generations after the life of the Buddha (as a disciple of the Buddha's son Rāhula) to the second century (as Nāgārjuna's guru), as is seen here. Nāgārjuna (approx. second century CE) is considered one of the most important Indian masters of Mahāyāna Buddhism. Śavaripa is considered one of the eighty-four Mahāsiddhas and a holder of the Mahāmudrā transmission. He was a student of Nāgārjuna and a teacher of Maitrīpa. Maitrīpa (986–1063), also known as Maitrīgupta and Advayavajra, was another prominent Indian Buddhist scholar and Mahāsiddha associated with the Mahāmudrā transmission. His teachers were Śavaripa and Nāropa. His students include, among others, Atiśa, Vajrapāṇi, Marpa, and Padampa Sangye.

4   These two streams of teachings were: (1) the monastic Kadampa tradition (Tib. transliteration: *bka' gdams pa*) founded on the basis of the Bengali master Atiśa's (982–1054) teaching activities in Tibet and (2) the yogic Mahāmudrā tradition, which Gampopa received from his root guru Milarepa (1040–1123). Gampopa was thus heir to a complex diversity of sūtric and tantric Buddhist views and meditative techniques. His great achievement was to integrate these different, and at times seemingly divergent, doctrines and practices into an integrated system of study and meditation.

5   The Karma Kagyü (also called Kamtsang Kagyü) tradition is one among the transmission lineages that were significantly shaped by Gampopa). In reference to him, these Kagyü traditions are often referred to as Dagpo Kagyü.

6   For precise explanations on this practice of Mahāmudrā see Shamar Rinpoche's book *Boundless Wisdom: A Mahāmudrā Practice Manual*. Edited by Tina Draszczyk. Lexington, Virginia: Bird of Paradise Press, 2018.

7   Karmapa Wangchug Dorje (1556–1603). Tib. transliteration: *karma pa dbang phyug rdo rje.*

8   Tib. transliteration: *phyag chen chos sku mdzub tshug*; Tib. phonetics: *chag chen chöku dzub tsug.* English translation: *Mahāmudrā, the Finger Pointing at the Dharmakāya.*

9   Tib. transliteration: *phyag chen ma rig mun sel*; Tib. phonetics: *chag chen marig mün sel.* English translation: *Mahamudra: Eliminating the Darkness of Ignorance.* Translated by Alexander Berzin. Dharamsala: Library of Tibetan Works and Archives, 1978.

10 Tib. transliteration: *phyag chen nges don rgya mtso*; Tib. phonetics: *chag chen ngedön gyamtso.* English translation: *Mahāmudrā: The Ocean of Definitive Meaning.* Translated by Elisabeth M. Callahan. Seattle: Nitartha International, 2001.

11 See note 1.

12 Tib. transliteration: *yi dam*, Sanskr.: *iṣṭadevatā*, is the "chosen deity" visualized and embodied in tantric meditation practice.

13 Guru Padmasambhava (8th c.), in Tibet also known as Guru Rinpoche, visited Tibet in the late eighth century. In various Tibetan sources he is usually depicted as a prince from Oḍḍiyāna in the northwest of India who practiced tantric methods. It is described that the Indian scholar-monk Śāntarakṣita suggested to the then Tibetan King Trisong Detsen (c. 742–800) that he invite this tantric yogi in order to subdue the hindrances Buddhism faced in Tibet. Having been active in Tibet for a while, Padmasambhava was forced to leave the country again, and it is said that he predicted trouble for Tibet and its Buddhists because he could not complete his activities there. Despite the various legends surrounding him, scholars generally agree that an Indian tantric master by that name did teach in Tibet in the eighth century. This is attested to in several tenth century manuscripts found in the caves of Dunhuang as well as in the early history of the imperial period in Tibet, the so-called Bashé (*dba'/sba bzhed*), the "Testament of Bashé."

14   Sakya, Tib. transliteration: *sa skya*. Literally, this translates to "greyish earth." It is the name of one of the major Buddhist traditions in Tibet that was established in the eleventh century by Drogmi Lotsawa (Tib. transliteration: *'brog mi lo tsa ba*), a disciple of the Indian master Virupa. Its main seat, Sakya Monastery in Central Tibet, was founded by Könchok Gyalpo of the Khön clan in 1073.

15   The first Karma Chagme, Rāga Asya (17th c.), who established the Né do Kagyü (Tib. transliteration: *gnas mdo bka' brgyud*) sub-school of the Karma Kagyü tradition. He received the Mahāmudrā transmission from the 6th Shamarpa, Mipham Chökyi Wangchuk (Tib. transliteration: *mi pham chos kyi dbang phyug*, 1584–1630), and was considered to have attained accomplishment through his practice on Jinasagara.

16   The actual title of this sūtra is: *The Mahāyāna-Sūtra of Three Aspects of Practice*, also called *The Sūtra to Purify Shortcomings on the Bodhisattva Path.* (Sanskr.: *Ārya Triskandham Nāma Mahāyāna Sūtra*; Tibetan transliteration: *pung po sum pa shags pe do* or *jang chub sems pe tungs shag*; Tibetan phonetics: *phung po gsum po bshags pa'i mdo* or *byang chub sems dpa'i btungs gshags*). As the practice is done with reference to thirty-five Buddhas, it is commonly also referred to as the *Sūtra of the Thirty-five Buddhas.* For a translation of this text see the booklet *Wisdom, Merit, and Purification Through the Blessing of the 35 Buddhas: A Text for Daily Practice.* Compiled by the 14th Shamar Rinpoche, translated by Pamela Gayle White. Potomac, Maryland: Bodhi Path Karma Kagyu Buddhist Centers, 2007.

17   Tangtong Gyalpo (Tib. transliteration: *thang stong rgyal po*) lived in the 14th/15th c. He was considered a great Buddhist yogi who also excelled as a builder of iron bridges, which is why he is also known as the "Iron Chain Maker." In fact, he is said to have built 58 iron chain bridges around Tibet and Bhutan, some of which are still in use today. He founded the so-called Iron Chain lineage of the Shangpa

Kagyü school, recognized the first Samding Dorje Phagmo, Chökyi Drönma (1422–1455), the female incarnation lineage of Vajravārāhī. He is closely associated with the Kagyü, Nyingma, and Sakya traditions.

18　Tib. transliteration: *bskyed rim / rdzogs rim*; Tib. phonetics: *kyerim / dzogrim*; the two processes of meditation in the context of the Yoganiruttaratantras, i.e., the highest Buddhist tantras.

19　The "four extremes" pertains to philosophical views that hold phenomena to be: (1) existent, (2) nonexistent, (3) both existent and nonexistent, or (4) neither existent nor nonexistent. The "eight elaborations" pertains to views that take phenomena as something that: (1) arises, (2) ceases, (3) is nonexistent, (4) is permanent, (5) comes, (6) goes, (7) is multiple, or (8) is single.

20　See Shamar Rinpoche's instructions in this regard in his *Boundless Wisdom: A Mahāmudrā Practice Manual.* Edited by Tina Draszczyk. Lexington, Virginia: Bird of Paradise Press, 2018.

21　There are a number of translations of this treatise. See, for example, *The Bodhicaryāvatāra.* Translated by Kate Crosby and Andrew Skilton. Oxford: Oxford University Press, 1995.

22　The so-called Four Preliminaries are: (1) refuge, developing bodhicitta and prostrations; (2) purification practice through Dorje Sempa recitations; (3) generating merit through maṇḍala offerings; and (4) receiving inspiration through guru yoga practice.

23　See the booklet *Wisdom, Merit, and Purification Through the Blessing of the 35 Buddhas. A Text for Daily Practice.* Compiled by the 14th Shamar Rinpoche, translated by Pamela Gayle White. Potomac, Maryland: Bodhi Path Karma Kagyu Buddhist Centers, 2007.

24　For detailed instructions on lojong, see Shamar Rinpoche's book *The Path to Awakening. A Commentary on Ja Chekawa*

Yeshe Dorje's Seven Points of Mind Training. Edited and Translated by Lara Braitstein. Reprint, Delphinium Books, 2014.

25 See Shamar Rinpoche's instructions in this regard in *Boundless Wisdom: A Mahāmudrā Practice Manual.*

26 For details on this, see the partial English translations of Karma Chagme's text in: (1) *A Spacious Path to Freedom: Practical Instructions on the Union of Mahāmudrā and Atiyoga,* and (2) *Naked Awareness: Practical Instructions on the Union of Mahāmudrā and Atiyoga.* Both translated by Alan Wallace. Ithaca, New York: Snow Lion Publications, (1) 1998 and (2) 2000.

27 Śrāvaka is the term used for Buddhist practitioners who do not follow the Mahāyāna. Nowadays, this approach of Buddhist practice is mostly referred to as Theravāda, which, even though it actually denotes a particular tradition, seems to have become a broader umbrella term.

28 Spiritual development in the śrāvaka system is usually divided into four stages of attainment: the level of a stream-enterer, a once-returner, a non-returner, and an arhat. Here, they are correlated to spiritual development in the Mahāyāna, where the stages of accomplishment are described by way of the so-called five paths: the path of accumulation, the path of application, the path of seeing (first bodhisattva bhūmi), the path of cultivation (second to tenth bodhisattva bhūmi), and the path of no-more-learning. The path of seeing is equivalent to the first so-called bodhisattva bhūmi in which a bodhisattva has attained direct insight into reality and is therefore liberated from saṃsāra, in that rebirth is no longer triggered by karma and afflictions but by compassion and wisdom. From then on, by virtue of the realization attained, they deliberately manifest in samsaric worlds to benefit sentient beings.

29 At this point, Shamar Rinpoche also went into a brief explanation of what "human being" and "celestial being" refers to: "How do you identify human life and heavenly life? A

human life is defined as an individual who can communicate and understand, whose faculties are clear, and who can explain or understand profound subjects like Dharma in words. Moreover, humans are not terribly under the control of bad karma. Heavenly life (in the desire realm) is similar, but of much better quality. These two are the useful lives for the path toward enlightenment."

30 These are the first two of the so-called five paths of spiritual development: the paths of (1) accumulation, (2) application, (3) seeing, (4) cultivation, and (5) no-more-learning.

31 There are a number of translations of this text. See, for example, *The Jewel Ornament of Liberation: The Wish-fulfilling Gem of the Noble Teachings*. Translated by Khenpo Konchog Gyaltsen Rinpoche. Ithaca, New York: Snow Lion Publications, 1998.

32 The entire *Treasury of Knowledge* consists of ten books with different sections that have all been translated into English. The section Shamar Rinpoche refers to here is contained in book number five, chapter 3: "The Commitments of Awakening Mind." In the English version, it is contained in vol. 3, pp. 161–213. This vol. 3 has the title *The Treasury of Knowledge. Book Five: Buddhist Ethics*. Translated by Kalu Rinpoche's Translation Group. Ithaca, New York: Snow Lion Publications, 2003.

33 Sanskr.: *praśrabdhi*; Tib. phonetics: *shinjang*; Tib. transliteration: *shin sbyang*.

34 Common name: grass of lucky augury; botanical name: *Poa cynosuroides Retzius*.

35 Shamar Rinpoche adds: "As you might know from the repetition of mantras, for example, when practicing on Dorje Sempa."

36 As an example for terrible consequences of ignorance and wrong views, Shamar Rinpoche gave the old "sati practice" in India, where widows burn themselves in the funeral pyres

of their deceased husbands. He described a legend in which it is said that a rich and ugly Brahmin scholar had such strong attachment to his beautiful young wife, that, driven by his jealousy and lack of compassion, he invented the sati practice, saying it was virtuous, because he could not bear the thought that she would re-marry after his death. The legend reports that this is why he wrote a book where he praised this sati-practice as a special religious and virtuous deed leading to rebirth in heaven. This practice became widespread in India.

37 Regarding the booklet with the translation, see note 14.

38 For a list of these see the appendix in Shamar Rinpoche's book *Boundless Wisdom: A Mahāmudrā Practice Manual*.

39 This text is available in the Bodhi Path centers.

40 That is, the first bodhisattva bhūmi and thus direct realization of emptiness.

41 Kriyātantra, or Activity Tantra, is the first of the three outer tantras. Along with meditation, this level of practice greatly emphasizes rituals, ablutions, and specific requirements such as special diets, etc. The Upatantra or Ubhayatantra, or Practice Tantra, is the second of the three outer tantras; it is also referred to as dual tantra and links the view of Yogatantra, which is the third outer tantra, with the Kriyātantra. The Yogatantra does not emphasize ritual purity; in meditation, practitioners view themselves as inseparable from the deity. The three inner tantras are the Mahā, Anu and Ati Yogatantras. While the first of these emphasizes the generation process, the Anu and Ati Yogatantras focus on the perfection process.

42 A collection of so-called terma texts in Tibet. They are considered spiritual treasures originally hidden by Guru Rinpoche or Padmasambhava and revealed by tertöns, that is, masters with the spiritual capacity to realize their meaning and transmit them further on to others.

43 Tib. transliteration: *gcig shes kun grol*; Tib. phonetics: *chigshe kündröl.*

44 Tib. transliteration: *khrid.*

45 This is the short form of a longer title. The longer title is *Meaningful to Behold, Instructions on the Union of Mahāmudrā and Atiyoga*, Tib. transliteration: *Thugs rje chen po'i dmar khrid phyag rdzogs zung 'jug thos pa don ldan.* English translations of parts of it were published by Alan Wallace with the titles (1) *A Spacious Path to Freedom: Practical Instructions on the Union of Mahāmudrā and Atiyoga*, and (2) *Naked Awareness: Practical Instructions on the Union of Mahāmudrā and Atiyoga.* Ithaca, New York: Snow Lion Publications, (1) 1998 and (2) 2000.

46 Compiled by Shamar Rinpoche and published on the Bodhi Path website: www.bodhipath.org/curriculum/. This overview or summary is not as detailed as the instructions given by Shamar Rinpoche in 2004 and puts a particular emphasis on the practice of *lojong*, or mind training. For contextualizing this practice, please refer to the more detailed explanations given by Shamar Rinpoche in Part I. Moreover, Shamar Rinpoche's book *Boundless Wisdom* on the practice of Mahāmudrā, in which he provides additional elucidation and support, was published only after his passing away and is therefore not explicitly mentioned here in Part II.

47 *Gateway to Knowledge.* Jamgön Mipham Rinpoche, vols. 1-4. Translated by Erik Pema Kunsang. Kathmandu and Hongkong: Rangjung Yeshe Publications, 1997-2012.

48 There are a number of translations of this text in English. One which also includes the Tibetan and the translation of Mipham's commentary on this treatise is: *Speech of Delight. Mipham's Commentary on Śāntarakṣita's Ornament of the Middle Way.* Translated by Thomas H. Doctor. New York: Snow Lion Publications, 2004.

49 *Abhidharmakosabhasyam of Vasubhandu,* vols. 1-4. Translated into French by Louis De la Vallée Poussin. English version by Leo. M. Pruden. Berkeley, Calif.: Asian Humanities Press, 1988-1990.

Publishing finished
in June 2020 by Pulsio
Publisher Number : 4009
Legal Deposit : June 2020
Printed in Bulgaria